VETERANS UNCHAINED

Breaking the Chain of Trauma
One Link at a Time

Presented by Gina Baker Alderman

ISBN: 979-8-8336-5133-9

Published by: Best in Business Publishing, LLC

Library of Congress Cataloging – Publication data has been applied for.

ASIN: B0B1CZG8GZ

ISBN: 979-8-8336-5133-9

PRINTED IN THE UNITED STATES OF AMERICA.

DEDICATION

This book is dedicated to the military women who went before us and to those who follow in our footsteps. Thank you for your sacrifices and for your service. We salute you!

#womenwhoserve

To all the families and friends who have lost a loved one to suicide. May this book provide encouragement, hope and support.

#22nomore

Contents

INTRODUCTION

Over 245 years of military service, women have served in every war our country has been involved in, starting with the Revolutionary War in 1775. Disguised as men, women served during the Civil War in 1861. In 1901 women were allowed to officially enter military service as enlisted nurses in the Army, and in 1908 the Navy created the Navy Nurse Corps. Women served in World War I and World War II as nurses, administrative support, telecommunication operators, and as pilots at home and abroad. Women pilots made up nearly eighty percent of the ferrying flying missions, delivering over 12,000 aircraft during World War II.

In 1948 President Truman created the Women's Armed Services Integration Act into law, which officially allowed women to serve in all military branches. Women nurses officially joined men in combat during the Korean War in 1950. In 1960, women served in Vietnam, with approximately eleven thousand women stationed in the combat zone. The first women graduated from the United States Service Academies in 1980 and in 1983 four female military police officers deployed into active combat. Over one hundred women served in Grenada in 1983.

As the Persian Gulf War unfolded in 1990, thousands of women served alongside their male counterparts and for the first time in military history, servicewomen were held as prisoners of war. Women took on multiple combat assignments, including flying into combat, leading troops, and fighting. Throughout the 1990's, women's duties included shipboard combat missions, fully integrated military basic training and in 1998 the first woman took command of the Navy's oldest commissioned ship, the USS Constitution. Over the last twenty-two years, women's roles have increased to encompass all military occupational specialties, including the elite special operations, combat ships, and submarine service at sea. More than 300,000 women have served in Iraq and Afghanistan since 9/11, with over 9,000 women earning the Combat Action Badge. Women currently make up 16 percent of the United States Armed Forces.

The nineteen women veteran authors in this book have had multiple tours in Iraq, Afghanistan and forward deployed areas around the world. This prestigious group includes an Army Inspector General Sergeant Major, a Navy Command Master Chief at sea, a Navy Captain specializing in forward-deployed Medical Plans and Operations, and nine women with full military retirement benefits. Each one of these nineteen authors have worked at the tactical, operational, and strategic levels of warfare.

Military service often comes with challenges that are unexpected and unplanned. These challenges can come in the form of experiences that are traumatic and life changing. Trauma can affect any human being at any given moment, and there are some that are at greater risk simply due to the nature of their occupation. Military service members, law enforcement officers, firefighters, and first responders fall into this category due to the stressors and requirements of their job. However, there are some specific populations of people, who may be exposed to trauma at particularly higher rates or be at increased risk for repeated victimization, such as women, children, those with special needs, and the homeless. For some populations, co-occurring issues and unique adversities can complicate recovery from trauma. Faith, God's grace, commitment, and perseverance all contribute to overcoming trauma to live fulfilled lives. Veterans Unchained is an anthology that shares stories of how 19 Military Women Veterans broke the chain of trauma one link at a time. It is their hope that these stories inspire others and help stop the 22-a-day military and Veteran suicides.

Gina Baker Alderman

Visionary Author

1 FOREWORD

By Sheila Farr

BEARING TRUE FAITH AND ALLEGIANCE

Courageous. Noble. Honorable: just some of the adjectives used to describe military service members. Throughout most of the United States, military service comes with a guarantee of respect because these individuals step up to display courage, bravery, and a sense of selflessness. Americans often thank service members at every opportunity for defending our freedom because young men and young women risk their lives to protect and defend the United States. At the time of enlistment, they take an oath to defend the Constitution of the United States against all enemies, foreign and domestic and pledge to bear true faith and allegiance to the same. This promise obligates them to have full confidence, belief, and loyalty in the execution of protection. Many are willing to die for their country, which reflects their noble character. Without those who are willing to sacrifice, we would not be free. However, we often forget about the trauma that can accompany our service members. Because they go places and see things most people could never comprehend, they are sometimes plagued with troublesome burdens; mental and emotional scars that they carry with them for the entirety of their lives.

Within the pages of this book, you will find stories from women who, with great faith in the power of healing and allegiance to belief that each of us belongs to a sisterhood of support, share powerful stories of their experiences with trauma, the military, and their struggles with overcoming obstacles post military service. These are stories of resilience, determination, and inspiration. They are reminders that even when our past haunts us, hurts us, and challenges us – we can still rise up to be victors in life!

During one of our pre-publication writing meetings, one of the authors (thank you, Hope!) lead a discussion about Kintsugi. Kintsugi (golden joinery), is the Japanese art of repairing broken pottery with lacquer dusted or mixed with powdered gold, silver, or platinum to give new life to a broken vessel. As a philosophy, it treats breakage and repair as part of the history of an object, rather than something to disguise or even discard. This not only teaches us to practice calmness when we experience unexpected breaks; it is a reminder of the beauty of human fragility as well. In a world that so often prizes youth, perfection, and excess, embracing the broken and battered may seem strange, but the 15th-Century practice of Kintsugi is a reminder to stay optimistic when things fall apart and to celebrate the flaws and missteps of life. We are all beautifully broken vessels that have purpose and value, for it is our brokenness that allows the light to permeate both from without and from within.

I would like to express my gratitude to the women of Veterans Unchained for their commitment to healing and helping others to do the same. Visionary Gina Baker Alderman has assembled a team of powerhouse veterans who come from all walks of life yet share the same story: you are an important and valuable member of society who has a unique set of gifts to share with the world!

Well done and thank you, ladies! Your courageous stories will inspire the world!

Sheila Farr

U.S. Air Force Veteran

About Sheila Farr

Sheila Farr is the CEO of Gulf Coast Training & Education Services, LLC, where she helps entrepreneurs and small businesses turn stumbling blocks into stepping stones by developing personalized business and marketing strategies that work.

Sheila is ABD for her doctorate degree in Organizational Leadership and holds masters' degrees in both Health & Wellness Counseling and Adult Education. A multiple time international best-selling author, in 2020, she founded Biloxi Reads!; an initiative designed to coach low-level readers and get books into the hands of underserved populations along the Mississippi Gulf Coast.

When she's not serving others in business, she's serving her community as a literacy and mental wellness advocate, providing job training as the Workforce Readiness Director for the Gulf Coast Human Resource Association and Mississippi's State Council of the Society for Human Resource Management, advocating for suicide prevention as an Ambassador for Mission 22, and writing her inspirational blog, "Thankful & Blessed 365."

She lives on the Mississippi Gulf Coast where she teaches yoga, Tai Chi, enjoys gardening, biking, and all things tea-related! You may connect with Sheila through her company's website at www.gulfcoasttraining.org

2

FAITH AND LOVE...STRONGER THAN CANCER

Esther Burlingame

U.S. Navy Veteran

"What gives me my strength?" That is the question people often ask me. I was named after Esther in the Bible, a woman with purpose; and grew up believing that I was created for a purpose. I am a child of God, wife, mom, grandma, daughter, friend, veteran, and cancer survivor. I served five years active duty and 28 years in the Navy Reserves. I was a Chief Hospital Corpsman in the reserves when I got my commission in the Medical Service Corps. Struggling to balance my military and civilian careers, family, and health. Life has taught me to build on my foundation of faith in Jesus with humility, courage, perseverance, and kindness. Looking for the silver lining in every cloud, it's important to accept and ask for help and prayers from family and friends. It is the only way to break the chain of fear in life. In sharing my story, my goal is to provide hope and encouragement to others who may be facing difficult life challenges.

At age sixteen I was blessed by God. My gift was anaphylactic shock! I remember looking down at my body, watching the medical team working on me. This near-death experience gave me the personal assurance that this life is not the end. I claimed Philippians 1:21 from the Bible: "For to me to live is Christ and to die is gain." Though suffering and pain remain, there is no fear of death, humanity's greatest fear.

At 33, I felt on top of the world. Married to the love of my life, mom to 3 rambunctious boys, the oldest six and four-year-old twins, working part time for a proprietary software company and as a lieutenant in the Navy Reserves. Our family was living the American dream. How quickly life can change. Three months after my annual physical I found a lump in my breast. After a benign result from the fine needle biopsy, I wasn't concerned going into surgery to remove the lump. I was laying on the operating room table waiting for the results of the frozen section to come back. Suddenly, my world was turned upside down. The surgeon was telling me it was cancer and that he needed to take more tissue to make sure that there were clean margins. The tears were running down my cheeks. I was praying to God to let me live to see my children grow up.

I spent a lot of time praying and bargaining with God and continued to work and drill because I didn't want cancer to run my life or cause me to lose my career. I asked countless people to pray for me and even when my boys got sick, I managed to stay healthy. When I finished all my chemotherapy and radiation treatments, I tried my best to put it all behind me, but like most traumas it is easier said than done.

I remember one night talking to my husband that I was considering a prophylactic (preventive) mastectomy. He couldn't understand why I would even be considering it. He desperately wanted to protect me and keep me safe, yet he couldn't see the enemy we were fighting. Invisible enemies are tough and the saying that we tend to hurt the people we love is so true. My faith, family and friends were the glue that kept me together.

During this time, I began to speak about the importance of self-breast exams and early detection to save lives. I remember how good it made me feel when a friend who heard me speak, credited me for saving her life after she found a lump that ended up being breast cancer. It's so important to learn to listen to your own body and to be familiar with your own lumps and bumps so that when something is different you can talk with your healthcare provider.

The next curveball in life was when we received a call from our son's school because he had a seizure at school. I hadn't realized that some of his unusual movements had been partial seizures. He was a real trouper, taking medications and having restrictions on what he could and couldn't do. As a mom, I prayed that he would be okay. It was so much harder to have someone I loved go through a medical challenge than it was facing my own challenges.

A little under three years after finishing my radiation and chemotherapy treatments I was on my annual two-week Navy Reserve training when I noticed a small lump under my arm. I knew that was not a good sign and was almost paralyzed with fear. I saw the doctors when I got home, and they confirmed that not only had the cancer come back it had spread to my lymph nodes. Since I was young (only 36) and had young children, I wanted to look as normal as possible and would need a mastectomy. Since I had already done radiation therapy, a breast implant was not an option. If I wanted breast reconstruction it would have to be a TRAM flap, where they take your transrectal abdominal muscle and use it to construct your breast. Like many women, I had complained to God about my "twin skin" (the extra belly skin created by carrying twins) and how I would like to get rid of it. God answered my prayers with the TRAM flap. Be careful what you pray for! I was in the operating room for over 12 hours and during the surgery I coded (my heart stopped). I vividly remember how sore my chest was following surgery and learned that it was because they had to perform CPR on me in the operating room.

This time I had to undergo more aggressive chemotherapy and take a leave from work and the Navy Reserves. Even with all the medications to prevent nausea and vomiting I was frequently throwing up and violently ill as the red elixir (Adriamycin) was being pumped through my veins. Getting ready for my next treatment, I couldn't help but think that I was getting a small glimpse of what Jesus must have gone through as he prayed in the Garden of Gethsemane the night before he was arrested and crucified, knowing what he was about to go through. I didn't want my boys (my oldest 10 and the twins 8) at the time to remember it as a year that mom was sick, so I fought hard to find the silver lining in this dark cloud. Having a focus and purpose outside of myself was key in finding the courage to continue. As Jesus demonstrated his love for each of us, I was learning that if I focused on others, my own battle was not as overwhelming. My faith and the love of Jesus was helping me make it through this time. This is a letter I sent to friends that year shortly after having my mastectomy, it is still true for me today.

May 18, 1999

My dear friends,

I woke up this morning at 0400 because I realized that God has given me the greatest gift of all – life. God has laid it on my heart that I need to share with my friends and family why I have such a great peace and "sound so good "even after all I've been through.

God has provided me a peace that passes all understanding. This is his promise to anyone who trusts their life is in the hands of the creator. I know that God has prepared a mansion in heaven for me. I have no fear of death because I know without any doubt exactly what waits for me on the other side. I believe the Bible to be the inspired word of God. It is His word that provides me with love, joy, peace and so much more.

I also believe that someday we will all stand before God and have to acount for how we have lived our lives and how we have served Him. God loves each one of us so much that he sent His son Jesus to die on the cross for our sins. It is my trust and faith in Jesus as my Lord and Savior that carries me through. I know many things are done in the name of Christianity that makes me sick — the ethnic cleansing in Kosovo is one of the current examples of things being done in the name of "Christianity."

It is my belief that each of us has a need in our life to believe in something greater than ourselves because I believe in Jesus Christ and the entire holy Scriptures (and yes I know anyone can take things out of context and twist it around to meet their beliefs.) I have a personal relationship with God where I can claim His promises and He has seen me through.

May the God of hope fill you with all joy and peace as you trust in him Romans 15:13

Love, Esther

I knew that the recurrence of my cancer would make it a challenge to be able to stay in the Navy and that I would be facing a medical review board. I didn't want to lose my Navy career, so I set out to prove that

I could still do everything that was required, including being able to perform sit-ups for the physical readiness test. My doctors had said this would be enormously challenging after having a TRAM flap since I didn't have the muscles usually needed to do a sit-up. The hospital corpsman at the reserve center wanted to process me out instead of helping me navigate the Navy's medical rules and regulations. I had to research and prove that the standards that she was referencing were those used for new accessions (recruits), not someone who had already been in for years. I researched articles, had my physicians write letters, and got other letters of recommendation as to why I should be allowed to stay in. In the end, the packet I submitted was over 50 pages. Finally, I received a response and was immensely relieved when it came back saying I was "fit for duty". Sometimes you must fight for what you believe in.

All during this time, I was constantly encouraged by friends, family, and physicians. I could always find people who were in better shape than me as well as those that were in worse shape than myself. When 9/11 happened, people suddenly realized that they could die without any warning. Everyone had just become more aware of the world that I had been experiencing, a world in which we don't know how long we live and that only God knows how many days we have on this earth. One of the silver-linings of life that my cancer has shown me is that it has forced me to look at, evaluate my own life and realize what is truly important to me and to realize every day, no matter how bad it seems, is a gift.

Since then, our family has continued to face many medical challenges and has seen many answers to prayers. My son, who underwent brain surgery at age 12, is now cured of epilepsy. Shortly after I returned from my deployment to support Operation Enduring Freedom, I had another regional recurrence of breast cancer and then several years later, lung cancer. Through all of this, I learned to trust God, ask others for help and prayers, and that helping others helps me. I managed to stay in the Reserves and with the support of family and friends, I achieved the rank of Captain (O6), before I finally retired to focus on my civilian career and family.

Striving to keep cancer "minimized on my screen of life" I was looking forward to being cancer free for ten years. Honestly, I had put cancer behind me. Then I fell and broke my arm, and the break wasn't healing. I was experiencing numbness and tingling in my arm. Thinking the break had impacted a nerve and I might need surgery; I had some tests. The tests showed that the cause of my numbness and tingling was cancer in my brachial plexus. I entered the world of metastatic/advanced breast cancer where they can't remove the "cancer" and there is no cure.

I am extremely blessed by the many medical advances that have been made in the treatment of cancer. They are providing a higher quality of life, and longer life giving me the opportunities to experience more of life's silver linings and to pursue my life's purposes as a child of God, wife, mom, grandma, daughter, friend, veteran, and cancer survivor. It is my faith in God, love, and support from family and friends that continues to be the source of my strength. Living with cancer, I know that when I am gone, it will be because my work on earth is finished. I am at peace knowing it is in God's hands.

My Chain Breaking Words for You:

For God so loved the world, that He gave His only begotten Son, that whoever believes in Him shall not perish, but have eternal life.

John 3:16

About Esther Burlingame

Esther Burlingame is a child of God, wife, mother of three boys, grandmother of seven, daughter, sister, friend, veteran, and cancer survivor living with metastatic breast cancer. An ardent veteran and patient advocate, she is a friend and mentor for those facing medical challenges. She had reached the rank of Chief (E7) Hospital Corpsman when she received her commission as a Medical Service Corps Officer. She retired from the US Navy reserves as a Captain (O6) after 33 years of service (five years active duty and 28 in the reserves). She spent 40+ years in the medical field and has been the recipient of several awards for professional articles. She is now integrating her passion and skills in writing about her personal experiences to bring faith, hope, and healing to others.

3

SILENT OBSERVER

Courtenay Nold

U.S. Navy Veteran

The truth, I think, is I am afraid to tap on the glass that surrounds me convinced the slightest crack in my psyche, my life, might shatter the glass and I will be exposed naked and defenseless to the sounds...the triggers...the constant barrage of 'outside'...I wish there were only 'silence,' only 'peace'...my reflection would be scattered in shards on the ground reflecting only pieces of my true self laying alongside dry blades of grass.

Unfortunately, it's the voice of a military member, young or old, that often goes unheard, lost in the shuffle of rocket attacks, daily tasks, leadership challenges and so much more...being pulled in all directions. It may seem like a quiet voice in a large room...falling on crowded ears. It may be a loud voice where no one is listening, preferring to pass by the voice without a look, notice or care. Sometimes it is hard to figure out what to say to a military member who is suffering from anxiety and depression. Often the only solution is them going home but that is not always possible due to different assignment requirements or needs. Serving in a high-paced and stressful environment can actually feel comfortable, especially for someone with multiple deployments.

I had acupuncture once. It was a group session at a VA. They ushered around 15 of us into a very small room. First mistake. Second mistake is they closed the door. They only had one doctor who went around the room placing the 'needles' into each of our ears. As the room grew hotter, I grew more and more claustrophobic. I wanted to walk out from the first moment I entered it after I saw the crowd in there. The only saving grace was finding a corner where I could see everyone and protect my back at the same time. The 'needles' were ones that looked much like tiny piercings and would fall out or could be taken out within a certain period of time. I waited my turn while I tried to avoid arm-to-arm contact with the guys sitting on either side of me. As soon as allowed/finished I shot out of that room, just short of a full-blown anxiety attack, and quickly left the building. Any benefit that I was supposed to feel was completely lost due to the nature and circumstances the session involved. I am pretty sure that I wasn't the only one who felt the way I did. That doesn't mean that acupuncture doesn't work. It just means that particular way of doing it doesn't work...at least not for me personally!

As John Donne said, "No man is an island"...no one on this planet...and, I would hope that every single serviceman and woman in this world has someone else watching their six (watching their back). When we return from service we come back to a world focused more on individualistic attitudes and more solitary existences than the close and connected, team-focused atmosphere we served in. We departed the 'hug' of our comrades-in-arms, expecting the same feeling on our return and simply not finding it unless we were lucky enough to remain in the service, remain with at least some of the same people we deployed with, or connect with like brothers and sisters through Veterans groups, group therapy, motorcycle clubs, and the numerous other outlets available for this very purpose. This most important thing is not giving up...and finding the right path to recovery for each person...and that it is never the same for all Veteran's. I very strongly believe that innate personality plays a strong role in this as well...as you cannot get someone who is introverted go out to a bar or dancing when that's the last thing they'd ever want to do...just as you probably aren't going to have an extrovert who likes spending time reading alone in a library.

One time when I walked outside with my hubby to go to the gym to work out we were met with a blast of cold air mixed with the sounds of heavy machinery and the smell of exhaust and all three wrapped themselves around me like a scarf in the wind, binding my senses tightly and depositing my mind and body back in Kandahar where these 'elements' were a normal occurrence. The chill in the air was what hit me first, numbing my face to what would come next. Because of my reaction I remained silent during the entire walk to the gym...mainly, I think, because I was trying to process what I was thinking and feeling; more importantly I was trying to reconnect with the present and ensure myself that I was in a safe place and not navigating the dusty, loud, smelly and chilly streets of Kandahar Airfield. The cold air initially took my breath away, somewhat like how you feel when someone knocks the air out of you or when you feel like you can't catch your breath. Quick breathing immediately followed, and I worked to control it by trying to consciously slow down my breathing...which took a while. The further away we got from the noise and smell triggers the easier it got to recover.

I remember feeling embarrassed every time I read or heard about service members who lost a lot more than I did while in a combat zone. By lost I mean that they lost arms, legs, eyesight...things like that. I didn't lose anything from my time in Afghanistan...except I lost myself. I don't see that as a deserving 'loss' though and that is why I am embarrassed. I don't feel like I deserve to say, "Yes, I lost me" because there are so many Veterans who lost a whole lot more and who seem to have gone on with their lives without a hitch, at least from my perspective. I recall walking through the hallways where I worked in Afghanistan. The plywood walls were mostly vacant but were interspersed with doors that remained open a majority of the time when I was actually at work. The thoughts of what would happen if our building were hit by a rocket attack was always present in my mind, especially since our offices were in a two-story building. I always thought that the building was more likely to be a target because of its increased visibility, being that it was a two-story building. I had to push those thoughts down deep...way in the back of my mind...to go about my daily business and take care of things. It was at night, in my 'rack', when those thoughts would resurface and keep me awake. This was especially so because there was often an increase in rocket attacks at night and I pretty much expected to be woken up (if I even was sleeping) by rocket attacks every night.

The question of my own personal faith, or rather of anyone's personal faith, I feel is something that each person must figure out on their own and not (for the faith to be true), be forced upon them. Recovering from the invisible wounds of combat is always difficult but, when you are able to follow clear steps towards that recovery with the support of religion, the journey can be at least a little easier. Faith helped me to better understand my new needs, as opposed to my former needs. Finding the path to peace is the objective and it's forward, not back. My own PTSD made me unable to recognize how war had changed me and what I needed to do to improve my quality of life. My own religious faith helped me to accept those essential truths. Of course, that may not be your experience.

I didn't know I had problems with PTSD until they became overwhelming. Shortly after my return from Afghanistan I attended a Navy Legal Officer training course, and I found myself sitting in a stuffy classroom and holding my breath. Gripping the edges of my seat, I tried to prepare myself for the loud clanking noise and the accompanying earthquake-like vibration beneath my feet. Sporadic but jarring, the noise was coming from the elevator shaft just outside my classroom. Everyone else in the room seemed totally oblivious to the noise and vibration. Perched on the edge of my seat, I braced myself as I tried to predict when the next impact would occur. I fought to stay in my seat and not run from the building. Waves of nausea hit me, and threads of tension spread throughout my body as my head throbbed and I stared at the course book, trying to read the same paragraph I'd already read several times before. The sound of metal against metal at the bottom of the elevator shaft sounded like a giant stack of weights on a workout machine amplified tenfold. I spoke to one of the instructors after class in the first week, explaining what I was dealing with and how short a time it had been since I was in Afghanistan, but the instructor didn't seem to 'get it' and I knew any conversation with the other instructor, based on my experience with him, would be about as useful as making a peanut butter sandwich with a toothpick. While I still made it through to the end of the class, I am amazed that I didn't stop coming altogether.

One thing that still very much bothers me...something that I am pretty sure will always bother me because I see no path to resolution...is the time that I had to be brought back to life with a crash cart. Of course, I wasn't 'there' nor aware of anything when it actually happened, but I found out about it a year and a half later. My Navy doctor never told me it happened. My attorney did when she found mention of it in my medical record. Now every time I see a television show, movie, or anything else on television or the big screen that relates to having to use a crash cart to shock someone and bring them back I think about what happened to me. I imagine looking down at myself from above the table, where they were shocking my heart to bring me back. What could have happened is they might not have brought me back at all...my heart wouldn't have started back up, and I would never have known any different. It would have been the same as if I had actually followed through with suicidal ideation...I just wouldn't exist. The only difference is that, in one situation I wasn't responsible, and in the other I would have been. In one I would have no excuse and in the other I would. This is a major source of anger for me, as well as disappointment, and it's the reason that it takes a lot for me to trust any doctor.

I am still in the process of finding my own path and sometimes just feel completely lost. The heat of the sun above barely heats my face, and I am in the bottom of a hole. The only way out is to claw my way up through the dirt, but it crumbles in my hands and falls at my feet. When panic attacks and nightmares don't let me sleep at night I return to that dark hole, furtively clawing my way upward. When I am overwhelmed and digging myself out of that hole, filing in under my fingernails with dark, moist dirt, I know nothing changes, like what I am trying to do is pointless and that my thoughts are taking me nowhere. Having to be in one of those places won't help me, or at least I won't admit that it will. My whole life, but especially so in my military and my civilian federal jobs, you are always expected to do your job well, with minimal assistance, and to ask for help only when absolutely necessary. When I was in Portsmouth, I was supposed to be able to get the help I needed so I could get better but all it really seemed like was that I was on hold and not making any progress. All I felt was that I was no longer good enough...that I was a disappointment...and why should I deserve to be around...especially when so many more didn't get to return home after their tours at all. Still more were exposed to roadside bombs, IEDs, accidents, rollovers, firefights and so much more and received Traumatic Brain Injuries, loss of sight, loss of limbs, and even suffered the loss of those who served alongside them, their brothers and sisters-in-arms. And I am still down there in that dirt pit, trying to figure out why my chest feels like I am holding a bowling ball on it...why I can't claw my way out, why there is no one up there at the opening who understands or believes what I am dealing with.

I had to get used to my own PTSD and its related triggers, so that I could continue to function on a daily basis. One thing I recall from deployment was walking in my combat boots, the gravel shifting under foot, mixing with the sand that was ground to the consistency of baby powder, covering everything with a cloud of dust. Shielding my eyes, I can still feel the rumble of the trucks approaching underfoot. I still have the same reaction here at home, feeling and hearing the trucks and trying to manage my reactions until I can get away from the noise. My heart-rate spikes and my palms get sweaty if I can't get away from noises like that quickly enough. Like the ignorance of others...some individuals who set off fireworks around the 4th of July; not even thinking about how the sounds and sights of the explosions bother those who served in a war zone. My tension drags me forward and, with blinders on, I try my best to ignore the sounds and my reaction.

I have issues with thunder and lightning as well. This is especially true at night, and I think it's because of the combination of the darkness with the sounds of thunder and the lightening...and because nighttime...in the darkness...is when a majority of the rocket attacks took place when I was in Afghanistan. It is especially bothersome to me when thunder is close enough that I can feel the vibration under my feet. Every movie that has action in it...for instance gunfire, bomb detonation, airplanes or helicopters taking off or landing, any overly loud noises, and even the scraping sound of chairs being dragged across the floor....I have to fight to not leave the room. I get the same reaction from alarm bells, music played too loud overhead, voices from loudspeakers, honking vehicles, police cars, fire engines and ambulances. This also happens when people are yelling or arguing, or even talking overly loudly...and whenever I am in any place where a lot of people congregate, I try to deal with my issues but often find myself inching towards the exit without realizing that I am doing so...as happened at my little sister Sarah's wedding reception. I feel like I am right back on base in Kandahar, my senses fully activated in that moment but totally absent to the present. The wedding ceremony was over with and everyone in the room seemed to be talking at once, clamoring for photographs. The dull roar that was produced triggered me and I was half-way out the door to the wedding 'chapel' before I even realized what I was doing. Even listening to my car's radio within a year of my return from deployment was impossible. I prefer absolute silence to even favorite songs that I used to sing.

I learned to deal with things as they come. For me it's like PTSD is an acquaintance who you learn how to put up with...to deal with. From the political side of things however, I am not always so understanding. One situation that I always have issues with is when publicity outweighs humanity just for the sake of the news ratings or individual prestige. There was a time, when I was working for a not-for-profit that assisted homeless Veterans (HVAF of Indiana - www.hvaf.org), that it was arranged for me to go with one of the Outreach Coordinators to visit one of the homeless Veteran camps. The coordinator took a lot of supplies including blankets, food with pull off lids, socks, soap and gloves. Once we get to where we were going, and the Veteran wasn't there at the time, the coordinator put the supplies in the vet's tent, and I looked around the area. To this day I wish I could have done something to fix things...but as I discussed with my co-worker, some of the Veterans flat-out refused to come in out of the cold. I had previously done a number of volunteer events to collect blankets and the like for these Vets...and during one such collection I was able to get a huge donation of U.S. Navy wool blankets. As I looked at that ragged tent, the layers of blankets and comforters stood out like a patchwork of layers on the tent roof. And layered over the rest was one of my large and very scratchy wool blankets...acting as a final layer to protect the Veteran from the elements...coming full circle from its original purpose. That wool blanket brought it all home for me...and was part of the inspiration for me to not only tell my story, but for me to layer a patchwork blanket of stories from my fellow Veterans...always choosing to take a chance and help others to find their own hope, even if that hope was to be found on the inside of a tent close to the VA.

I didn't get a lot of sleep during my deployment and there were times that I would work all day and part of the night and just forget to eat. I don't know what the reason was, but I just wasn't hungry in the slightest and I was constantly busy with no slowing down, so I guess it was just too easy to forget. The military also provided me with the perception of a framework of loyalty and dedication to service. When my career came closer to being over, however, that perception was replaced with disappointment and distrust. I didn't feel I belonged anymore. I was in a Navy that I no longer felt I could call my own. When I go to VA appointments, I find a majority of the Veterans in my peer group or younger with severe issues and even missing limbs. A lot of them have some level of Traumatic Brain Injury (TBI) from various types of explosions or weapon related events.

Even though I have a TBI diagnosis, I don't belong, or rather I don't feel like I deserve to stand alongside those who got TBI in other ways. I got it either during ECT treatment or when I coded during an ECT procedure, making it necessary for them to use the crash cart to bring me back. The result was Brain Lesions. Because of my memory and communication issues I can frequently be repetitive, and am easily frustrated, often prompting people to tune me out. Older Veterans seem to carry themselves with more of a sense of pride and I can think of no other reasons but the eras they belonged to and the support and friendship of their fellow Veterans. Other than the possibility that my uniform might not fit (due to medications identified later that caused weight issues), I have been very uncomfortable with the thought of wearing my Navy uniform at all. I also don't feel as much a part of the Navy team any longer because of the way I had to leave the Navy.

I often worked 16-hour days, if not way more, during deployment. To tell the truth, I really have no idea how much I worked...but it was nearly always dark when I left. There were at least daily flight line announcements for Ramp Ceremonies, honoring our service members lost in battle. Even today when I think about the ceremonies, and the men and women laying inside those coffins, under their nations flag, and I hope that there is someone at home to support the remaining family. While I couldn't make myself, seeming to always find a reason because of my workload, to not go...but I knew what happened during these ceremonies. I found myself years later watching one of these ceremonies, that occurred more recently in Kandahar, Afghanistan, and laying my fingers on the computer screen, and found my fingers followed the coffin as it was carried from the plane to the hearse...and I felt tears welling up in my eyes for the first time in years (since my own Afghanistan deployment actually) and a tingle running down my spine. I shiver even now thinking of this...because I watched it over and over again (so many times I lost count) and felt the same way every time...I still do. It doesn't matter that I didn't know that service member. It never does and it never will. Just that fact that it was someone who served our country...who died in service to our country...and that's all that matters. I am embarrassed that I wasn't able to set the example and honor our lost by attending while I was still 'in country' but I always made sure, when I was doing Casualty Reporting, that I received all required information and transmitted it to the appropriate entities so I could ensure that personnel would be properly recognized or taken care of in relation to combat related injuries. I was often called a 'Bulldog' because of my stubbornness, but I wouldn't have been any other way. It was the only way I could be sure that 'my' combat injured personnel were taken care of.

One thing I enjoyed during my time at Kandahar Airfield was the USO tour performance and, more specifically, Robin Williams. Aside from an unexpectedly high number of 'colorful' words, his performance was top-notch. The only thing he said that seemed a little off was when he shouted, "Hello Kandahar!" and he just didn't seem to have the heart to back up his exclamation...to me he just seemed a little down. Even so, he told a lot of jokes and made it worth it to be there and was a temporary distraction to where we all were. The unfortunate thing about the venue was that Army personnel were taking up all of the area close to the stage, making it difficult to get a good view to back up sound coming from the speakers surrounding us unless you brought binoculars with you. On the flip side however, before and during the performance I kept thinking that the entire area could be targeted, many military and civilians could be killed or injured, and, in my opinion, that the performance wasn't worth anyone's life. I remained on the fringes of the audience and left well before the show was over.

If I could have stayed in the military service I totally would have. I just had no choice in the matter. My experiences were varied...especially when I was in Kandahar. I guess it was nice that we didn't have to live in a tent but living in a building had its tradeoffs too. The local nationals who came in to clean our barracks bathroom always made me very uncomfortable. It didn't help matters at all, but my room was right next to the bathroom. My already jumpy demeanor was that much more so when the cleaning crew was there, and I often found myself involuntarily twitching my arms or legs. Since my bunk shared a wall with the bathroom, I could hear everything when they came in the building and started working on the bathroom. They were noisy but kept to themselves, so I wasn't sure if those actually cleaning were male or female. I just knew there was always a male supervisor. Other than the racket they made and them appearing at odd times, they always yelled before entering the bathroom to ensure no one was in there. This meant that the people close-by, like me, got to listen to the bellow of "housekeeping" before they entered the bathroom and went to work.

Having to struggle against your PTSD is one thing, but when you have physical ailments on top of it, such as almost constant migraines, or an assortment of physical pains or health issues, it is another thing altogether. In my case, I often have to deal with daily headaches that I wake up with and there is not much that helps me out with the issue other than taking a nap when they get bad...and sometimes that doesn't even help as the migraine is usually still there when I wake back up. It's just one more issue that limits my good days when I actually feel well enough to get out of the house. With the assistance of medications from the VA, some useful, some not, in addition to Migraine medication from the drugstore, and I can join the land of the living once in a great while and avoid living like the Gollum dragging myself out from the depths of a swamp, with the 'precious' golden ring of pharmaceuticals hung heavy on my neck...saying: "We swears to serve the master of the precious. We will swear on the...on the precious." - Gollum

I often found myself trying to do my best possible job, no matter what the circumstances were, while I was in the service. I always wanted to try and help others to be their best...in their careers...their lives...their health...pretty much anything. I still feel that way. Maybe sometimes maybe I care too much... but I have learned that sometimes I also have to let go...that I don't have to fix everything to validate my own life and my own self-worth. I also know that there are people out there who can help all of you out there who are dealing with PTSD. Remember that you come first, and you must be your own first priority no matter what.

Overcoming PTSD takes time, and for anyone who is or has experienced this, you know exactly what I mean. I liken the experience to a quote that states that, "The man who moves a mountain begins by carrying away small stones." – Confucius. For me, it seems like each small success, like each stone you carry, and then cast away, lightens your load just a little more and makes your life just a little easier. Your actions, your movement, your thoughts...all of those can bring about healing in your own life if you let them. You just have to be willing and ready to cast away the stones in your way. It is your choice to make this change and to let your own personal happen. Little by little, amazingly, you can move that mountain in front of you.

My Chain Breaking Words for You:

"Our greatest glory is not in never falling, but in rising every time we fall.

~ Confucius ~

Poems by Courtenay Nold

Accept the Rain

A broken chain lays on the ground.
Shattered links of trauma found.
Hands forever freed from pain.
Face lifted to accept the rain.
Opened eyes with faith...I see.
Who escaped with hope...it's me.

Into The Light

Out of the darkness
And into the light
Reaching out a hand to you
No one should walk alone
Along the dirt path of trauma

Focus your eyes despite the dust

Of memories left unsaid

Releasing the pain within your soul

Roaring out from blistered lips

Echoes of anguish reverberate

Then die away

Let the darkness go

Focus on what gives you peace

You no longer walk alone

I've got your six

Promises To Keep

Stars are for wishes

No matter how many

Your thoughts brush the stars

That shine like new pennies

And reach ever upwards

For heaven they seek

They came from your mind

But you've promises to keep

Promises to keep

For your hope still to go

You remain here on earth

Thus, to help those you know

And your wishes become blessings

Planting the seeds...seeds of love not despair

In the hearts of your friends and those who live here

And some others...sans wishes...their will you defend

For sometimes their dreams just float in the sky

Held close to the earth by pain nobody should bear

But with a fisherman's net cast way up high

You pull down some wishes...to wish for instead

Peace in their lives and love in their souls

About Courtenay Nold

Courtenay Maria Nold cares deeply for others, and especially for those who, like her, are dealing with PTSD and Moral Injuries. Guiding others to find their own path to recovery is of vital importance to her. She calls what she does, "Daring to make a change...any change."

Along with that focus on changing lives, she has written a very well-received and free eBook titled Total War on PTSD, an anthology of sorts, that features 45 chapters by experts in their fields who donated their expertise to benefit those suffering from PTSD. This eBook currently has over 150 downloads to date. This free eBook is available by going to www.bn.com and looking up the title 'Total War on PTSD.' She chose to offer it for free to facilitate helping as many Veterans, First Responders and civilians as possible.

She holds a Bachelor of Science in Organizational Security and Management. She is the author of a book of poetry (thus far unpublished). She is also a certified Paralegal. She served in the U.S. Navy and Navy Reserve for almost 15 years, as both an enlisted Yeoman and an Administrative Officer.

She manages the PTSD Resource Group on Facebook as well as promoting her free eBook and sharing motivational quotes and images on her account page. Her motivation is to help as many people with PTSD as possible and strongly advocates that PTSD, in any form, and from any cause, is not the fault of the person involved.

PTSD Resource Group page:

https://www.facebook.com/groups/ptsdcptsdresourcegroup

Courtenay Nold account page:

https://www.facebook.com/profile.php?id=100076081372051

You can reach Courtenay via e-mail at courtenaynold@att.net or can follow her on either of the Facebook pages shown above.

4

I AM MY SISTER'S KEEPER

Amarin Trichanh

U.S. Army Veteran

What does it mean to be a sister's keeper you ask? My name is Amarin Trichanh, an immigrant from Bangkok, Thailand. I honorably served in the U.S Army as a logistic specialist and combat medic healthcare specialist for thirteen years and I am a disabled combat veteran. I am the youngest of three girls. My sisters and I are four years apart. Although I am the youngest I always felt overly protective of my two older siblings. When I was just five years old, my parents took us into a refugee camp. This was during the early 80's when France, Canada, and the U.S were taking refugees from Laos, Cambodia, and Vietnam through the refugee program.

Refugee camp was much like a prison surrounded by barbed wires. There were refugees from Vietnam, Laos, and Cambodia. We were all patiently waiting to be manifested into the lists of families that will be fortunate enough to migrate out of the God forsaken camp and onto the plane to a new land of freedom and opportunity. Each family was being sponsored by relatives from wherever they were heading to. For my family, it was the U.S, San Diego, California to be exact. Life as a refugee child was full of trauma. I mean, sure I made a lot of friends, but for some strange reason I became really ill. It was a combination of really bad asthma and uncontrollable whooping cough that eventually led to my spitting up blood. I was always weak and was never healthy like the other children.

For a total of two years, everyone lived in fear because the refugee camp was run by corrupt government officials that abused their power and got away with everything and anything such as murder in broad daylight, violence, kidnapping, and rape. I have seen it all. I lived in fear that these low lives would hurt my family or kidnap me to be sold and trafficked to child sex

slavery. Although I was only seven, I knew what all these things meant, and I was constantly afraid and having endless nightmares. Two years I lived like this along with my illness. I was constantly weak and coughing up blood. My first sexual trauma experience happened at this one schoolhouse. I was young and innocent at the time. I started first grade really late so at this time

I was already seven years old. Some of my friends were telling me that there was this really nice man giving out ice-cream money to the kids and that I should go get ice-cream money too. I was really curious, so I went over to this one part of the schoolhouse to see who the man was. When I got there I was creeped out and picked up a bad vibe especially when the man called me over to go and sit on his lap. I hesitated and backed away as the man came closer reaching out his hand to me. Something told me to run, but the skinny creepy man caught me and picked me up and locked his arms tightly around me! I started yelling for him to let me go as I kicked and struggled I remembered he reeked of alcohol and this pervert was trying to grab and grope me while tightly locking one arm around me. Up to this day I was so thankful that I was a tomboy and a real fighter. That sick bastard tried to pin me down and rip my jeans open. I punched him in the eye then got one leg loose and kicked him between his legs and took off running. My heart was pounding so loud! I was bruised and scratched up, but thankful I got away.

It wasn't long until my friend's parents found out about that creep. One day I witnessed him getting jumped by a group of men and he got tore up pretty bad. I witnessed so much death and violence during my time in refugee camp and that was what led me to want to become a soldier later on in life. I wanted to be a protector of the innocent and fight bad guys. I hated bullies and I saw the way women were being dragged off and raped in broad daylight. I remember wishing I was an adult at the time so I could fight and help all those innocent people in that hellhole. I couldn't wait to get the hell out of there and finally be free and not live in constant fear or live in a confined environment like a bunch of prisoners. Nineteen years later I enlisted in the U.S Army post 9/11. I figure it was time for me to give back to the country that gave me a new home, freedom, and a new life. It took me a while to decide, and I wished I enlisted after high school, but better late than never. I was twenty-six at the time. I left for basic training April 10,

2002, filled with motivation and dedication. I was ready to be the best soldier I could possibly be. I initially started out in the California National Guard for the first four years. Slowly and surely my love and faith in the Army started to fade away as I started noticing toxic leadership and the way most of the men only regard their female counterparts as nothing more than an object or eye candy. I immediately became disgusted when I found out that a bid was placed on me for $200.00 for whoever was the first guy to sleep with me.

The only guy I cared about and trusted betrayed me and lied about being single only to rip my heart open before deployment while to throw salt on my wound, as I was grieving from that betrayal, I was drugged and sexually assaulted by another service member 5 days before being shipped off to Iraq. I had no one to turn to. Hardly anyone! In my whole entire thirteen years of service I can count on one hand how many women had my back. Why is that?

Why can't women come together and protect one another instead of hating and competing for the attention of these men that clearly don't give a damn about us?

I had a friend who was a female soldier crying to me that she was set up to be raped by another female soldier. This is unacceptable! We have to do better! Look at the cases of Private First Class LaVena Johnson and

Specialist Vanessa Guillen! We have to do better! We have to have each other's back.

Ladies, what does being a sister's keeper mean to you? Well, here is what it means to me:

The love between sisters
Together through hell we fought
The bond is everything
Whether we're blood or not
From all walks of life

No matter the color of our skin

We're all related through love

That radiates from within

We are all created beautifully

Unique in our own way

Respect we give one another

Each and every day

When we sisters stick together

No one will ever lose

Everyday we love and praise one another

Hatred we will not choose

We clap and congratulate

When our sisters succeed

Now this is the kind of love

That everybody needs

Everyone will get a turn

If we keep working as a team

Supporting one another

As we live our dreams

I will always have love for my sisters

I will never let you down

Anytime you need uplifting

I will fix your crown

I will be my sister's keeper

I will be your voice

I will be the strength for those

Who no longer has a choice

Steadfast and loyal I will remain

Next to my sister's side

I AM MY SISTER'S KEEPER
Until the day I die

If we women stick together, how powerful will that be? While we are created beautifully we are also powerful and strong. We are the ones who give birth to man. We are the nurturer, the teacher, and the guardian. We are the epitome of resilience. We are warriors that have been chosen as survivors of trauma to tell the stories of how we have risen from the ashes. Hear me, my sisters. Hear me as we come together to bond and heal so that we can become even stronger than ever before. We are survivors and we will never hide our scars.

The world is filled with wonder
Although life may not be kind
As we enter the battlefield we realize
Our lives are on the line
Everyday is a constant struggle
Just to stay alive
In this deadly battlefield
Only the strong survives
Where is your battlefield
What are you fighting for
What have you overcome
Fighting these endless wars
There will come a time
Where there will be endless nights
But the faith within our hearts
Will show us the light
Fear is our worst enemy
Battle that demon from within
Put on that armor and believe
That you will always win

We may become weary

And wounded 'til near death

Never cease don't ever surrender

Until your last breath

And if the enemy is our mistakes

That leaves some scars behind

May these be lessons learned

Let it be a sign

To become a stronger warrior

A reminder of why we fight

Or why we must keep moving

Before we start losing sight

Of the true meaning

Or what these wounds stand for

That just because we're wounded

Doesn't mean we lost the war

Society believes that beauty is flawless

But these markings define

Inner beauty and strength

The legacy that's left behind

These wounds they tell stories

Of courage and survival too

From all aspects of life

We never even knew

Don't ever be ashamed

And hide your battle scars

It's your one legacy that defines

Who you really are

I must say God is so good to me and I am grateful to be alive so that I could share my stories. I am grateful that I don't ever have to feel alone or ashamed anymore. Coming from an Asian background, I was sick and tired of everything being my fault. Everything was always my fault every time something bad happens. It's like I always had to be so perfect all the time, but somehow I was never enough. I was not good enough for this, not good enough for that and I was bullied for being ugly. Growing up, my parents were constantly moving, trying to put me in the best school, not realizing that it was hurting me in the long run and I fell into deep depression. After a while I had problems fitting in hence tossing me into a group of misfits. I became angry. I got into fights at school, then it was detention, skipping school to having an abusive relationship and getting pregnant at eighteen. Things just keep getting more and more messed up so I just gave up and dropped out of school altogether. What a shame and embarrassment I was to my parents. People started judging and telling me I would never amount to anything.

Well, guess what? I am something today. I am someone today and I will continue to be. No one knows us better than us. Don't let anyone tell you that you will never be something in life when you know you can. Healing takes time. Everyone is different. Take it one day at a time and never allow anyone to set a timeline for you. I have been through hell and back in my life and have attempted suicide too many times. I have been stuck in the darkest place and I have been hospitalized. I am in a much better place now and I intend to stay here. I have done it and so can you.

My Chain Breaking Words for You:

Take it one day at a time and never allow anyone to set a timeline for you.

About Amarin Trichanh

Amarin Trichanh was born Tapee Vorachak on November 16, 1975, in Bangkok, Thailand, the youngest of three girls. She immigrated to San Diego, CA with her family through the refugee program on August 17, 1984, when she was 8 years old, hoping to secure a better future for the family and better education for her. When Amarin completed her education, she wanted to repay the United States for her freedom and new life, so she enlisted in the U.S. Army after 9/11 at the age of 26. For the first four years of her enlistment in the California Army National Guard, Amarin honorably served her country as a patient admin from April 9, 2002, to January 13, 2015. For the next four years, she served in the active Army as logistic specialist, and finally as a combat medic healthcare specialist her last five years of her Army career. Amarin has completed two combat tours in Iraq (Operation Iraqi Freedom III, Operation Iraqi Freedom VII) and one tour in Afghanistan (Operation Enduring Freedom). In addition to her military service, Amarin's passion combines writing, learning new languages, fitness, arts, and crafts. Amarin has dedicated her life to advocating for and inspiring others to follow their dreams and help spread love, peace, and kindness. She is also an activist for victims of MST (military sexual trauma) and advocate for the Me-Too movement.

5

GOVERNMENT PROPERTY

Brandi Miles

U.S. Army Veteran

I never wanted to be that girl that screamed sexual harassment. I always thought that I was in a man's world, so I just kept my mouth shut and drove on like any good soldier would. Honestly, it really wasn't that bad to me because my stepfather trained me well!

I'm just trying to figure out how to speak about this in the right way so that it does not affect a lot of people and people can understand where I'm coming from when I speak about these things. I want to help other people understand my perspective and help other women that are going through some of the same things that I've gone through. I didn't really understand myself or know myself until I became a life coach. Before becoming a life coach, I feel like I was always in survival mode from day to day, hour by hour, minute to minute. Survival is a natural reaction when humans are locked down and controlled by something that they don't think they will ever get out of. I adapted very well in the military environment; the controlling, the organization, the structure - all of it. Before, I couldn't understand why I adapted to it so well! You see I've always felt like I've been controlled by the government in some way or another and that's why I believed that I have always been "Government Property" until now.

Now that I'm a life coach I'm a lot more aware of my life and how everything unfolded. I can look back and see how it was so easy for me to adapt to the military environment. It was an environment much like my home was growing up. One that is very strict, an environment where refusing a command would cost you dearly. One where you don't own anything, especially your body and how it was so easy for me to adapt to the military environment of men being in control. A lot of people don't know this about me, but for the first eight years of my life my mother was married to a man that was in the military. He was a drill sergeant and he sexually abused me for the first eight years of my life. He molded me into what he wanted me to be, he controlled everything about me, even as a young child. He controlled how I dressed, how I cut my hair, what I ate, how I cleaned my room (military style). He was even more controlling sexually, depending on the mood he was in when he got home from work. I know it's pretty sick to think about, but this sexual abuse helped me make it through the military a lot easier than for other women, because it was normal for me. It was normal for a man to touch me in a sexual way. It was normal for a man to speak to me in a sexual way. It was normal for a man to play sexual and mind games, and it was normal for a man to try to control me when I wouldn't do what they wanted me to do. It was all too normal for me!

When I first joined the military in 1998, I can remember in Basic Training our Senior Drill Sergeant took all of the females in a room and stated that his Drill Sergeants did not want us and that we should never assume that they do. But at the same time several of the drill sergeants were putting myself and my battle buddy in the front leaning position; that is when a drill sergeant would have you on the ground completing some physical activity, so they could talk to us. By the middle of basic training, it got to the point where my buddy and I spent most of our time in front of our drill sergeants doing push-up, sit-ups, flutter kicks, planking: you name it we were doing it. We were in the front leaning position so much that my battle buddy and I maxed our physical fitness test at the end of basic training. Male soldiers would walk past and did nothing. Other drill sergeants would walk past and did nothing, and female soldiers would walk past and did nothing.

At first it was fun to me and my battle buddy because they were just talking to us, but as time went on, a few of the drill sergeants started getting more personal and controlling. One drill sergeant started a personal connection with both me and my battle buddy. He started controlling me like my father did. This felt normal to me, and he made me think that he really cared about me. He was my drill sergeant, and I just did what I was told, because my father trained me well. Later he and others were sentenced to a military prison for doing this to multiple girls that came through their training facility.

Throughout my life coaching experience, I've learned a lot about myself and how I operate. I read a book by Gary Chapman called "The 5 Love Languages," and I realized that he left one out. You see my mother wasn't very nice to me, so because of my father, my first love language was SEX. So, throughout my military career I just always thought that the guys were just being guys. I thought it was a compliment to be wanted and to have the attention. I was never "raped" in the way it's often thought of, so I wasn't worried about it. As I have worked through some of my past traumas, I can see how my stepfather normalized my childhood molestation, making me a prime candidate for harassment and assault in the military as an adult. In fact, I can remember several women speaking about sexual harassment and military sexual trauma, but I was always like one of the guys. Now that I look back, I can see the different perspective from a woman that has been through things like myself versus a woman that hasn't experienced that childhood trauma. I see that their military experience was a lot different than mine. I see now that it was a traumatic experience for a lot of women. I was sexually harassed and even assaulted throughout my military career, but I didn't see it at the time. It's sad to say, but that was the norm in the military culture and there were a lot of heads that turned the other direction when things were going on.

I don't think anyone should ever feel like they belong to someone or something. We all should own our bodies and our minds. Despite having been government property for so long, I am now my own woman. A woman who has turned her traumas into superpowers. Love, empathy, awareness, and strength are just a few of the things I have learned and use to help veterans climb out of that feeling of not belonging and into your own self again.

Now I see that I created superpowers to protect myself! My trauma heightened my empathic abilities. I can see someone's emotions very quickly, just by observing their body language or how they speak to me. If I felt a bad vibes from another soldier male or female, I just made sure I wasn't left alone with them. I made sure I had someone with me at all times when they were around. Now that didn't save me every time, but it helped to have that superpower of observation and awareness. This superpower also helped me protect several people in my life that I was close with. I could always sense harm a mile away because I have experienced much of what my clients have been through, I grow an exceptional bond with my clients. I am able to truly understand their pain and walk them through their healing.

Because of my childhood sexual trauma, I've been searching for true connection and love with others my entire life. Sometimes this has led to unhealthy relationships. If we are connected, male or female, I am very loyal to you. I love you and I am very protective of you. As I have healed, and become a Certified Life Coach, I can differentiate between trauma bonding and true bonding. I help my clients work on healthy relationships and boundaries as well. Leaving the military means stepping into a whole new world with zero safety net – be mindful that you aren't allowing your trauma to lead the way. I love being a life coach and helping others. To be able to be an ear, shoulder or even kick in the seat to so many veterans has been a joy I can't put into words. I am so grateful and thank God for the trust they put in me and guidance I give them.

Now I can see that everything that I've been through in my life has brought me too here and now. All of the good and all of the bad has brought me to here where I can help veterans move forward in their lives and help them start living their dreams!!

As I help my clients, they are also helping me just as much as I'm helping them! I have grown so much in the last three years. Going through the transition of becoming, facing myself, the good, the bad, breaking generational curses and - most of all - breaking the chain of my own trauma one link at a time. I still have a long way to go; it's a journey not a destiny! I believe God has given me the gift to help and heal, to use my trauma to be a blessing to others. I also believe that everyone has the ability to come back from brokenness and be something great no matter what they've been through – especially YOU!

My Chain Breaking Words for You:

To change from where you are, you must decide where you would rather be. Rosa Luxemburg said, "Those who do not move, do not notice their chains."

About Brandi Miles

Brandi Miles is a world changer – and she wants to bring you along for the ride. A mother of six, love is her superpower. Brandi is an ICF Certified Life Coach for veterans and a believer in the power of playing (which is evident in her signature tie-dye, well, everything). As part of the Mississippi Army National Guard for 16 years, Brandi helps veterans go from camo to rainbow. Brandi's clients learn how to view life differently and break free from fear that often makes veterans feel stuck. The guidance Brandi provides them after they leave the structured and controlled life they've known in the military is the key to unlocking their greatness. She uses her life experiences and education to provide them with support, encouragement, structure and advice.

Coach Brandi Miles is a #1 international bestselling author with the anthology, "Cage Fight," being her first published work. She tells part of her own story of leaving the military and coming to terms with her own feelings of being stuck. She has shared more of her experiences and story as a part of docu-series "Women in Combat," where she also served as the life coach on set. Brandi was then invited back to be the life coach on set for another production – a reality show called "A Little Love."

Brandi is beyond proud of her time with: 184th Sustainment Command, 3656th Maintenance Company, 298th Engineer Battalion, 106th Support Battalion, Deployment: 184th Sustainment Command, Kandahar Airforce Base, Afghanistan 2010-2011, MOS: 92A, Automated Logistics and 92Y, Supply Sergeant and love pulling from her own experiences to help veterans find pride from their experiences in the military.

You can reach Brandi for coaching, public appearances or speaking opportunities in the following ways: Phone 318-880-6871, Email: VeteransUnleashed1@gmail.com or you can follow her at @VeteransUnleashed or @CoachBrandiMiles on social media.

6

THE EVER-EVOLVING SOUL:
MY TRANSITION FROM
VICTIM TO SURVIVOR TO THRIVER

Dr. Shirley Boykins Bryant

U.S. Army Veteran

The trauma I suffered manifested itself in several forms, including profoundly distressing and long-term disturbing experiences, emotional shock following a stressful experience, and physical injury. The trauma I experienced included one-time, multiple, and long-lasting repetitive events. In addition, I displayed symptoms that could be associated with posttraumatic stress disorder (PTSD) while not formally diagnosed as such.

The impact of trauma was subtle, insidious, and outright self-destructive. Trauma-impacted me in a myriad of ways that included societal factors, my personal characteristics, the type and characteristics of the event(s), developmental processes, and the definition I placed on the trauma, and other socio-cultural factors (which means **common traditions, habits, patterns, and beliefs present in a particular group).**

My emotional reactions to trauma varied significantly when influenced by my socio-cultural history. Beyond the initial emotional reactions to the trauma, other emotions that surfaced included anger, fear, sadness, and shame. However, I did initially encounter difficulty identifying many of these feelings. First, I did not grow up in a family or community that expressed emotions, which led me to associate strong emotions with the past trauma, thus believing that emotional expression is too dangerous or would lead to feeling out of control (e.g., a sense of "losing it" or going crazy). There were also times when I flat out denied having feelings associated with the traumatic experiences and defined my reactions as numbness or lack of emotion.

For years after initial treatment, I saw myself as a victim and felt as though I was still in the trauma. In these times, the sense of being trapped permeated my feelings, thoughts, behaviors, and even affected my sense of self-worth. I suffered from having low self-esteem. I felt a sense of shame and worthlessness. During this time, I did not feel that I deserved nice things or deserved to be treated respectfully by others and had difficulty setting healthy boundaries. Subsequently, I became involved in dramatic and unhealthy relationships with toxic, unsafe people and often put my own needs last. I had problems communicating except in a passive or passive-aggressive manner. I was hypervigilant, always expecting a threat, and felt guarded, and even during the healing aspect, I often felt alone, selfish, numb, damaged, confused, and hopeless. I did not believe that my story was worthy of sharing for a long time. I felt overwhelmed by my past as I constantly relived the struggles I endured. I tended to believe that suffering was just the way things were, and I had difficulty finding happiness and making friends. I frequently turned to my drugs of choice, food, and alcohol, to help me feel like I was doing okay.

I knew that I was transitioning to replacing how I see myself from victim to survivor when I began to feel strong and confident and genuinely believe that there were resources and different choices are available to aid me with the healing process. I started moving away from unhealthy relationships and making unhealthy life choices like abusing food and alcohol, to making better choices like attending classes and seeking therapy. It was then that I recognized the struggles and could see the tools needed to strengthen my walk with God. It was then that I decided that no experience was a wasted experience as long as I learned from it. I knew that I had survived these events for a reason and decided that they would serve as a testimony for who I have become today. My grieving process took place in women veteran support groups. As I sat weekly with other women veterans who were often eager to tell their stories and wanted to talk about all the aspects of their experience in their attempts to heal. It was then that I felt a true sense of healing. Attending support groups served to be a significant help for me as I entered this stage. Through this process of sharing, I began learning ways to set healthy boundaries and explore what was safe or dangerous in other relationships. By attending this support group and sharing experiences with others, I began identifying patterns, and I then started setting goals to proceed with the changes I wanted to see. While the changes I strived for did not happen overnight, I did begin to see gradual progress in weeks. I began to note a shift in my mindset when I transitioned from believing that suffering is expected, to gaining a sense of hopefulness and confidence that I will survive this trauma. One day I started living what I thought was a healthy and everyday life with healthy relationships. I began to authentically laugh again and find the absolute joy that could only be found in a relationship with the one creator – God. Instead of needing food, alcohol, or co-dependent relationships, I learned to regulate my emotional pain and sought out a good therapist with whom I could explore the new and uncomfortable feelings that have been numbed or disregarded before. After years of attending therapy, I began to feel like I was starting to thrive!

There was still more to go on this journey – to that end; I began to see myself as a Thriver. It was here that I learned there is *"power in the words that we speak to ourselves."* I started to repeat daily affirmations and say positive words to myself. I began to pray and search biblical scriptures that addressed the thoughts and challenges I was experiencing. I gained a new sense of gratitude for this newfound life overflowing with miracles and excitement. Instead of feeling isolated, I began to feel connected with others and the universe. I have a new sense of pride in who I am and my ability to care for myself. I now focus on living and being fully engaged in the present moment and understand that emotional pain passes, and there is something to be learned from each experience.

Through transitioning to how I saw myself, I began to set healthy boundaries with others and protect myself from toxic people. However, I continued living with an open mind and heart. I learned to place my needs first as I recognized that helping others required that I care for myself first. It was here that I learned to create peace instead of allowing chaos.

As a result of my transitioning to the process of thriving, I began to display outward confidence and a feisty personality. I was not afraid of challenging work or trying something new. I have a life coach who keeps me focused on my present and future goals. I have completed my studies to earn a Doctorate in Human and Organizational

Psychology; I have served as a co-author to an Amazon international bestseller anthology titled, "The God-fident Woman." I am a co-author to a second anthology titled, "Stepping into Leadership Greatness," scheduled for release in June 2022. In addition, I have been featured in magazines for articles that I have written and served on panels as guest speaker and conducted workshops on team building. The sky is the limit for me, and I daily give GOD thanks for all he has done and continues to do in my life.

My Chain Breaking Words for You:

Jeremiah 29:11

" For I know the plans I have for you," declares the Lord, "plans to prosper you and not to harm you, plans to give you hope and a future."

Philippians 3:13

Brothers and sisters, I do not consider that I have made it my own yet; but one thing I do: forgetting what lies behind and reaching forward to what lies ahead.

About Dr. Shirley Boykins Bryant

Dr. Shirley Boykins Bryant hails from the great state of Texas. She is an Author, Behavioral Coach and Chief Operating Officer of Let's Talk About It - Behavioral Coaching, LLC, and Educating Our Youth, Inc., which is a non-profit organization.

Dr. Bryant has a Doctorate Degree in Human and Organizational Psychology; she is a certified Emotional Intelligence and Cognitive Behavior Practitioner and has a diploma in Modern Applied Psychology. She has written and published research titled, "The Lived Experiences of Federal Human Resources Professionals During the COVID-19 Pandemic," and co-authored an Amazon international best-seller anthology titled, "The GOD-Fident Woman."

Dr. Bryant is a Veteran of the United States Army, who retired at the rank of SGM after serving honorably for 23 years. Dr. Bryant's hobbies include spending time with her family, reading, and traveling.

7

TRAUMATIC GRATITUDE

Hope Baker

U.S. Army Veteran

It was three days before graduation for MP school at Ft. McClellan in 1996. I was in the bay shining my boots and a voice came over the loudspeaker, "Baker, report to the captain's office with a battle buddy right away!"

I had no clue what was about to take place; not one clue. I grabbed Williams and we headed down the stairs to the Quad, standing outside the battalion door at attention and reporting our arrival.

I was a late starter at 31 but had always dreamed of being a police officer ever since I was 12 years old. Back in my hometown where I grew up, I used to hang out at the courthouse where they had the dispatch office and talk to the cop on duty just listening to the calls as they came in on the scanner. I was fascinated with law enforcement work in every aspect, it was a passion of mine. The thing that kept me from it for so long was an early failed marriage and giving birth to my oldest daughter at the young age of 16, and then another marriage soon after to a man who fathered my three other daughters! So, in essence, I was a child trying to raise children.

My first marriage was just two high school kids thinking they knew more than they did, and after three years of fighting over the father not working, doing drugs, and hanging out with other women while we lived with numerous family members, I finally threw in the towel and told him to leave. The second marriage was a struggle from the start as well. I got pregnant and wasn't "in love" with the father but believed that I could grow to be over time, so I agreed to marry him. Over the course of six years in that marriage we moved numerous times; some of those times were evictions. In the beginning this seemed like a repeat of my first experience, my husband couldn't seem to hold down any job for any length of time and certainly nothing that paid well enough to pay the bills. It seemed we had a different car about every six months or so. He had a rock star dream of becoming famous in the music industry and his focus was on that so much that a lot of important things were neglected in our lives. I don't think anything is wrong with having dreams such as these, there just needs to be a balance so it doesn't destroy or harm others in the process of achieving them. We had three children of that period during all the moving, I attempted to go to college and majored in music. During the last semester of my second year, I gave birth to our last daughter. Becoming very depressed over all the turmoil of no stability, I just didn't go back to the college and officially withdraw from my classes, so I got all incompletes. I was also diagnosed with postpartum depression at that time. It took about a year of trying to dig myself out of this black hole that seemed to have swallowed me whole before I just couldn't go on like I was any longer. I felt like a caged animal about to do something so reckless and chaotic that I wouldn't be able to come back from whatever it was! I ended up leaving my entire family so I could get the help I needed.

After a self-admitted hospital stay, I filed for a divorce, got custody of all the children, and my father ended up helping me out while I continued working on my depression. I was in and out of the hospital trying to get to the core of my depression and one thing that was discovered was that I had a chemical imbalance and needed to be on medication. They said it was Bipolar depression and, in some cases, it could take a long time to get the medications right. My father lived on the east coast and offered to help by offering to take my two youngest daughters into his home assuring me that I would always be welcome. He just wanted me to be well again. I couldn't even take care of myself at this point, so I thought of the girls and did what was best for them. During one of my hospital stays, my second born wanted to go and live with her father and I knew that his family had stability at that time, and I was in and out of the hospital still trying to get my depression under control, so I let her go. My oldest daughter ended up going to live with a family friend in Texas during this time. I knew that I couldn't take care of these little angels, but I wanted to make sure they were taken care of, I had a responsibility to make sure they had homes with stability and people that could physically and mentally take good care of them. No matter how heart breaking it was for me, I had to do what was best for them and then focus on myself. After approximately four years of hospital stays and trying different medications, it seemed that the doctors finally found a combination of drugs that was working. My dad suggested that I come to live in South Carolina with them so I could start my life over. I could be close to the girls, and he would help me get my feet back on the ground again. This is what I decided to do because I felt it was best for the circumstances, for the children, and for me.

A routine was formed, and I was back on track and finally happy. I started looking into my future and what my options were with what time I had left for a career choice. This is when I decided to check into the Army and see what was available for me.

This was early 1996, I walked into the recruiter's office and met with Sergeant Hanover. He got me set up with everything and when it came down to my options Military Police was on the table! I can't even begin to explain how excited I was to even fathom the idea of my dream coming true. I mean, finally something in my life was going to be working in my favor and I would be set for life not to mention I would be able to take care of my children very well! My dreams were coming true!

I got signed up on the delayed entry program, that gave me time to get into shape since I was a little older than most going in. I mean, I was 31 and I would be going in with mostly 18-year-old girls, so I really had to step up my game! Sergeant Hanover worked with me so much, running and going to the gym working out with me on a regular basis until it was time to head out to MEPS. He was great, I felt he went above and beyond to help me be a success! My father and his wife were totally on board with this decision and thought it was a great plan for my life. They were already taking care of my two youngest girls and had no problem continuing to do so.

So, when the time came to go, I checked in at Fort Jackson in Columbia, South Carolina, at the MEPS station. That's where new recruits got sworn in and the whole process took place before going off to boot camp for my MOS. It was amazing that my sister, who was a Lieutenant in the Navy at that time, got to come over and swear me in! It was surreal! She really showed me a lot of support in my decision, and this was such a special time for us!

I'm not going to lie; basic training was truly a challenge for me. There were days I felt like giving up and I would lay in my bunk at night and cry and pray to God to help me and show me that I was where I was supposed to be. One morning I got up after almost giving up getting my Kevlar helmet to take it and the leather band that was supposed to fit around the inside of the helmet for comfort and stability to the drill sergeant's office so he could help me put it in place. I had all but given up the night before due to the exhaustion of the day and the long lines at every drill sergeant's door, I just couldn't go and stand in a line, so I turned in early to cry and pray feeling defeated. To my amazement when I pulled the helmet out of my locker the band was fastened tightly in place where it belonged, and no one had a key to my locker but me! No one even knew what had happened the night before regarding my defeat with that helmet! That was the sign that I was looking for! God showed up and showed out, so I had my proof that I was where I belonged in my life at this point. This was a true miracle that God gave to me, just for me!

From that moment on the struggle seemed easier. Every time the wind blew on my face it felt like God was kissing my cheeks, reminding me that he was with me. How could I fail with God beside me, and I'm sure sometimes, carrying me. Boot camp didn't seem so bad any longer and when it was over with, AIT school started. At Ft. McClellan, MP training was given at the same place as basic, so we didn't have any transition from one place to another. We also had Christmas exodus before starting the next phase so that was nice to get that little break. Home for two weeks and then back at it!

AIT school was interesting. Mostly we learned procedures on how to fill out paperwork. We did learn how to subdue perps of course and direct traffic, all the basic duties of the MP world. They say nothing can truly prepare you for the real deal, you must live that to learn it.

So, graduation was approaching quicker than any of us realized! This is where I get the call over the loudspeaker. We're told to enter the office and report to the captain. Battle buddy standing outside his door, me just inside at attention in front of him, he tells me at ease.

He looks me dead in the eyes and asked, "Upon entry did you disclose that you had any problems with depression in the past?" I had to answer that I did not! He asked me why and I disclosed that my recruiter had told me that if I had no issues with it upon entry then there was no reason to put it in the paperwork.

My Captain informed me that my ex-husband had just called him and asked why the United States Army was going to let a person with mental health issues walk around with a gun. My Captain was livid, but not at me, at my recruiter and at my ex-husband. Now this had to become a JAG issue. As it turns out, we learned that all the recruiter had to do was file a waiver in order to correctly place me in military service.

So, my dream of becoming a Military Police officer was stopped right there. I had to temporarily switch my MOS to S1, which was processing new recruits at the Military Police post, and this was going to be my duty station unless something changed! This was near to becoming a nightmare and let's not even talk about morale at this point. Can you imagine going into the Army to become a Military Police Officer and having this ripped from you only to process other recruits to have your dream job? At least I was given my own room on base and a patch for my uniform to show that I belonged somewhere. I wasn't allowed to have my car yet and I'm not sure what was behind that decision. One very positive thing about this experience was that I did get to graduate with my company, and I did receive my Military Police certificate, that was awesome by the way. My Captain said that I did the work and I deserved that, so he made sure to make that happen for me.

There just wasn't enough work in the S1 department because they were already maned with everyone they needed before I even came along. It was clear that the base was just trying to find a place for me where they really had no place and monitor me at the same time. I'm guessing they had a liability of some kind since we were dealing with depression and suicide in the military is at a high percentage already without bringing someone in that might be a risk, I understood to a certain degree. The word was that they were going to have me start driving the Sergeant Major around to all the new recruit exercises. I was apprehensive about that so much! One of the jobs they had me doing was cleaning the Sergeant Majors quarters and he was there many times and made me very uncomfortable. This just wasn't setting right with me at all. This had been going on for months and they just kept on jerking me around. I was starting to get depressed again which I know was exactly what they were looking for!

I ended up going home one weekend and just not going back. I just couldn't face another day of them not knowing what to do with me and me not knowing what they were going to do. I didn't want to drive the Sergeant Major around and I didn't want to get pulled down into a depression again, so I decided not to go back at all. I called my Senior Drill Sergeant the next week and told him that I wasn't coming back, and I apologized to him for causing him whatever trouble that it caused him. I had mad respect for him so that's why he got that call. I'm sure anyone who has been in basic training has at least one person in authority that they feel that way about, he was mine. I went on for several months as a bartender getting paid under the table until I decided that I had enough of sick people threatening to turn me in. I hired an attorney that was a retired JAG officer. He told me to go to Fort Knox and turn myself in. The whole process would take three days and it would be over with. He was right, it was just that simple and such a relief once it was done.

The thing I find the most interesting about the disturbance is that I was never mad at my ex-husband, not even from the first word from my Captain about him calling. I'm not sure exactly why. I immediately felt sorry for him and cried. It also showed me how badly I had hurt him in the past by leaving him and breaking up the family. I could only pray for him and ask God to forgive me for the pain I had caused.

I feel like I learned so much through this experience. I didn't accomplish the goal that I originally set out to reach, I reached something as equally important for myself, learning immediate acceptance and forgiveness. You see, I believe that everything happens for a reason even if we don't know what the reason is. This experience showed me that my faith in God is greater than anything. It made me a stronger person and for that I have a heart full of gratitude!

God had greater plans for me, and my story goes on and gets much better. Many of us have sad stories but for me it's what I learned and what I took with me from the experience that matters most. I have learned to live one day at a time and enjoy each moment as it comes because that is all we ever really have. Life is a gift, and each day is new and full of surprises to be discovered. I say enjoy and don't sweat the small stuff! Be in the journey!

My Chain Breaking Words for You:

"I can do all things through Christ who strengthens me." Philippians 4:13

A Poem by Hope Baker

Winding Clock

Winding clock winding down

Trying to stay somewhere on the ground

Ticking seconds, minutes pass

Working with the hourglass

Grains of sand passing through

Showing time to me and you
What will come we never know
What has passed will never last
Trying somehow to steal more time
What we've seen is so defined
Wishing, hoping, wanting more
Winding clock, as before.

About Hope Baker

Hope Baker works hard in a lab each day testing fabrics and yarns for customers such as Tesla and Hanes. She finds her job fascinating and looks forward to the daily process of seeing if the product can pass her quality assurance check list. After hours and weekends, she spends her leisure time with her best friend; her 9-year-old boxer/Lab fur baby named Emiko (which means "beautiful friend" in Japanese). Long walks on any Green Way they can find and all the dog parks available in the area are no stranger to her and her fur baby. What an amazing pair these two are and sure to make friends wherever they go. Looking on the horizon of adventure and true joy, they want to extend their journey by inviting you along to read a short story that was written by this young lady, a first-time author, in *Veterans Unchained*.

8

WONDER WOMAN COMES FULL CIRCLE
LEARNING TO LIVE WITH NEW
SUPERPOWERS

Loretta Connatser

U.S. Navy Veteran

My story is not unique. It is a story of a woman, who survived childhood trauma, dropped out of college, enlisted in the Navy, survived sexism, racism, and sexual harassment in the military, retired from the military and is working on living her best life possible. Forgetting, compartmentalizing, not trusting, and ignoring were some of my learned survival superpowers from childhood. Little did I know that eventually, in the right atmosphere like the military, my superpowers would be perfected to help me not only survive but thrive. One by one, traumatic events that I had forgotten slowly showed themselves as dreams or memories that I convinced myself were scenes from movies I had seen. My older sister, I'll call her "the Historian," was always willing to enlighten me. She would talk about something, and I never knew if it was my memory or hers. But this isn't a sad story; quite the contrary. It is a story of survival, strength, success and eventually forgiveness and healing. A story of a father and daughter's relationship. This is my story of hope. Hope that someone reads it, sees themselves, and realizes that they too can break the chains of trauma to learn how to live their best life.

I won't share a lot of specific events; there are too many. The few I will tell are to best help define him and our complex relationship. I will tell you that as a child, there was abuse including verbal, physical and sexual that I either witnessed or was victim of. Here's what you need to know about him; he was once handsome and charismatic, he is a Vietnam veteran, he was abused as a child, he abused drugs and alcohol and was at times homeless, he is presently bedridden in a nursing home, and he will die alone.

My first memory of him is him blowing pot smoke at me while I sat in a laundry basket, loud music blaring, and people laughing. He was the life of the party and I always wanted to be around him. I remember that Mom was rarely happy. There was a sadness in her eyes, which I think was sometimes fear. His personality would change instantly, and he would yell at Mom, my sister and me. It was nothing to get spanked. His favorite phrase was "go get me my belt" and "stop crying before I give you something to cry about." I remember him hissing these phrases at us as we stood in the kitchen doorway watching him beat Mom. All the while she was trying not to yell out in pain or cry so we wouldn't be scared. She was trying to defend herself but eventually she couldn't take it anymore and she told us to run downstairs and tell the neighbor to call the police. We ran downstairs and eventually the yelling stopped and she came down. Her eyes, face and hands were red and swollen. The Historian told me that once he stopped beating her, he apologized and cut himself in a suicide attempt. One of many attempts over the next decades. The ambulance and the police showed up. The police handcuffed him, put him in the back seat, and took him away. He didn't come home again for what seemed like a long time. Mom was battered but smiling; I was happy she was okay. She was always happiest when he was gone. After ninety days he returned from prison; so did his sporadic behavior, abuse, and apologies. Similar episodes continued over the next few years, even after we moved to Colorado. I was four.

I vaguely remember driving up to the big white hospital. We drove together as a happy family to meet Julius, his friend, whom I later learned was his therapist. Julius was short, had a big smile and an even bigger afro. To a four-year-old, he was silly and fun. I was happy because the darkness in his spirit seemed gone around Julius. Soon after we got home, the happiness left, and his darkness returned. After that, I hated the VA because it didn't help him. He kept hurting Mom, my sister and me. Eventually Mom found the courage to kick him out for good. She thought we would be upset when she told us that she was going to get a divorce and he wouldn't be back. I was happy. That meant that Mom and the Historian wouldn't be sad and scared anymore. I was seven.

Mom got a new job at Climax mine. We had more toys, health insurance and a truck. Mom was gone a lot though, even on her days off. The Historian and I were alone a lot, and we would spend some weekends at our cousins. My uncle abused my aunt too, but I felt safe around my cousins because there were six of us. Over the next few years, we would sporadically get his drunken late-night calls. I never understood why Mom always let him speak to us; she never spoke bad of him. I thought that made her weak. The Historian was always hopeful he would change; I learned that men don't always do what they say they will. I was twelve.

Mom finally met a good man who wanted not only her but her daughters too. They got married. He was caring and responsible, and he made Mom smile from the inside out. My new dad would go to my school events, and he wasn't abusive. It was easy to love him. Over the next few years, my new blended family survived the shutdown of the mining industry with alcohol and welfare. We all had part time jobs. After the Historian graduated and went off to college, I was alone for the first time in my life. I was rebellious as my parents focused their attention on me. I wasn't used to the new way of life with rules and adult supervision. Although my new dad was loving and attentive, I had already learned to distrust men. I sought the comfort of emotionally unavailable boys. Always feeling like I wasn't enough; always having a plan B just in case. When I graduated from high school, I was good in sports and math, so it made sense to go to engineering school on a sports scholarship. I didn't want to go but I wanted to please my dad and mentors. I was seventeen.

The Historian surprised me at one of my college volleyball games when she showed up with him. I played great and after he tried to talk to me. I was furious at her. I felt violated. This was my safe place and she brought him without asking me. He had no right to be a part of it, let alone sit up there with a smile like he had something to do with my success. He asked to speak to me when I was walking back to my dorm. I stopped and he had tears in his eyes and said something about being proud; asking how I was. I laughed, shook my head in disbelief and stood there not saying a word. I was eighteen.

Three years later when I was stationed in San Diego, his sister told me I might run into him since I was living close to the beach he frequented.

She was right. One day I was jogging, and I noticed him sitting in a car. As I passed, he yelled my name, so I stopped. He asked me how I was doing and if I was looking for him and had I joined the Navy because of him. I shook my head in disbelief; could this really be happening again. At that moment Big Loretta reassured Little Loretta that he couldn't hurt her anymore and I spoke my mind. I could tell by his expression that he was surprised that I talked to him in that tone. No one had ever stood up to him. He had always been the bully, but I wasn't afraid anymore. The Navy had taught me to have courage and to speak up for myself. At that moment I saw a change in his eyes; the tables had turned. I wasn't afraid of him anymore. I was a woman and a Sailor. I was twenty-one.

Over the next decade of my career, I perfected my superpowers, worked hard, and made a name for myself. I was home on maternity leave when the Twin Towers were struck. I called the clinic I was stationed at and told them to turn on the news. The operational tempo and mission of the Navy changed that day. We started augmenting the Army ground units with Sailors. The Sailors I served with and eventually led would see ground combat like that not seen since Vietnam. Seven years later, as a leader I decided I needed to volunteer as an individual augmentee with the Army. I wanted the firsthand experience to better understand what my subordinates were dealing with, and I felt like it would make me a better leader. I had no idea what I was in for. After I received my orders and made all the family arrangements, I called him. I don't know why. It had been fifteen years since I had seen or even talked to him. I tracked him down, and when he answered the phone, I froze. The scared little girl wanted to hang-up, but the Sailor in me sat there and spoke to him. It was casual. He asked what rank I was, he called me a kiss-ass. He asked why I was going to fight in a war that wasn't ours and I told him that I had volunteered, he called me stupid. At that moment I regretted calling him. He started yelling but refused to say anything about his time in the military. When the call ended, I reminded myself that I had no expectations and for the first time he had not disappointed. Later when

The Historian asked why I called him I couldn't come up with an answer; not one that I felt she would understand. I suppose I wanted closure just in case I didn't return. On my way to Afghanistan, Mom called and told me she had cancer. She told me not to worry and she would see me for Christmas when I safely returned. The next time I saw her, she was bald from her treatments but had her big optimistic smile. I noticed the scars on her bald head. When I asked her about them, she looked away with tears and shame. The Historian told me they were from him. Apparently, I had forgotten the time he had beaten her in the bath with a hiking boot. Mom just kept cooking when I cried and gave her a hug; she never spoke bad of him. I thought that made her the strongest person I knew. She died thirteen months later. I was forty.

I retired after twenty-five years and nine months of active-duty service. Injuries that I had downplayed and compartmentalized became obviously apparent. My superpowers were survival skills that the Navy reinforced; but I no longer needed to survive, I needed to relearn how to live. I needed new superpowers. I remind myself that I am not him every time I drive to the VA for treatment. The Navy took me out of my comfort zone and taught me to be confident and strong. With the help of my husband, friends, family, and therapist, I started doing the work to be healthy and capable to trust myself to have healthy relationships. In addition to the numerous doctor appointments, I found myself reading books, taking naps, and spending time outside gardening. I even drove my daughter back and forth to school. There were more bad days than good. I was forty-six.

Years later, I received a call from the VA in Phoenix. I knew he was in a nursing home in Arizona, and it triggered my superpowers; I didn't answer. After listening to the voicemail from Julian, his social worker and fellow vet, I found myself returning the call out of a weird, indescribable, sense of duty. Julian asked a few questions about him, so I took the time and explained a bit about our relationship and our family history. Not surprisingly, most of the information Julian hadn't known. I've never forgotten the abuse or the visible and invisible scars he gave us. My experience in life, the Navy and in combat taught me life is precious, and I was able to eventually find forgiveness to help my healing. This in turn, enabled me to move forward and communicate with him not as a daughter, but as a fellow veteran. I was fifty.

Now I call him every six months. When he asks me if he can come live with me, I tell him no. When he asks me to visit, I tell him no. When he asks me if he will see me again before he dies, I tell him no. I think the Historian still doesn't understand how I keep my boundaries with him. I tell her I use my new superpowers and our relationship is purely based on our military service. I'm proud of my service and the work I've done to heal, which in turn helped me break that link in my chain of trauma. I'm also proud of the work I continue to do every day to manage my old and newly learned superpowers including forgiveness, trust, and vulnerability. I now have more good days than bad, and I thank God every night for that. Truth is, it's not easy; it's fuckin' hard, but I know I'm worth it!

My Chain Breaking Words for You:

Sometimes life brings you full circle to places you have been before just to show you how much you've grown. Remember: If it was easy everyone would do it.

About Loretta Connatser

Loretta Connatser is a 25-year Navy veteran. She served at various duty stations including three overseas tours, Fleet Surgical Team 4 which deployed twice aboard USS Kearsarge (LHD-3), and a tour in Afghanistan as an individual augmentee as the NCOIC/OPS Chief with the Cooperative Medical Assistance team, Combined Joint Task Force-101, during Operation Enduring Freedom. She was born in Los Angeles, CA and was raised in Leadville, CO. She has two adult children and lives in Virginia Beach, VA with her husband Bill, who is also a 31-year Navy veteran. She enjoys spending time outside with her dogs in the garden.

9

THE BEST REVENGE IS A
LIFE WELL-LIVED

Stephanie Ann Grant

U.S. Army Veteran

I stood there in front of the Colonel's desk, my legs feeling like they were going to give out at any moment. This was the last place I wanted to be, and I was alone—no one here but the Colonel and myself.

"You brought shame to all the women who served before you," He thundered. I wanted to slip into the floor right there. I wanted to cry, but I didn't. I couldn't. I could feel the anger well up inside me like I'd never felt before. Hot coals burned in the pit of my stomach.

I remember saying NO, I don't want this! WHY am I being punished???

"You are an embarrassment to the United States Army." Those words inflicted pain almost as intense as the actual rape itself. Since they came from my superior officer, they must have been true, right? I guess I had to stand there and take my punishment.

It was just the Colonel and myself, but it felt like God's Judgment against me. I never felt so alone. As the Colonel looked at me, there was a mixture of anger and a hint of pity in his eyes as he met my own.

"Well, what do you have to say for yourself?" He waited for me to respond, but I couldn't. He was my leadership, and he failed me. Deep down, he knew that me getting gang raped was not my fault, but he couldn't allow a scandal like this to come to light.

It was far easier to blame me, the victim, because it was my squad leader and a handful of other individuals' words against mine. It was just a few days just before Christmas in Iraq. I reported to a squad meeting that night, which wasn't unusual. I could trust these guys; we had been thousands of miles on the roads in hostile territory. They were all like brothers to me, or so I had thought. That all changed that night after our pre-mission meeting. Someone brought a case of beer to the meeting. Drinking was strictly forbidden, but some people still found ways to obtain alcohol. Where there is a will, there is a way to get just about anything; you just had to have the right connections. I was offered an open can of beer, even though I was hesitant.

"Go ahead; it's just a beer. We're all grown adults." One spoke. Okay, why not? He had a point. I took the beer and took a drink. I had to admit; it tasted good after not having one for almost a year. Then I started not to feel so well. The next thing I remember was feeling out of control and having my squad leader on top of me. I remember crying a lot because this was against everything I ever stood for.

"No, I don't want this! Please stop! stop!" I begged. "Come on; you know you always wanted this." MY squad leader said while he was on top.

The rest of the details were a complete blur, but I was in and out of consciousness. I admit that when it comes to drinking, I'm a lightweight. However, I have never blacked out drinking like this, especially not from just one beer. Someone must have roofied it.

The following day, I woke up in total pain all over my body. I heard whispers and giggling in the ranks in formation. Overnight, I was transformed from a shy girl into a slut. Yep, to this day, I still don't remember everything that was done to me, but I don't want to know. It doesn't matter anymore. I wanted to speak with a chaplain badly but was advised not by higher leadership.

"You don't want to incriminate yourself by admitting that you drank alcohol against orders." I was told.

It was true. If I hadn't broken the rules in the first place, I never would have been in this predicament. Did the punishment truly outweigh the crime, though? It wasn't even a whole beer; it was a taste of one.

Aside from the physical pain of being gang-raped, those I thought I could trust betrayed me in the worst way possible. If you ever want to make someone feel worthless, you rape them. Let me tell you; it's pretty damn effective.

After deployment, I thought I was no worse for wear. I found myself getting angry or tearful over small things. It felt like the whole world was against me. I made unhealthy choices, allowed myself to be manipulated by others, and isolated myself. Getting punished for being raped was something I thought was acceptable at the time because that's what good soldiers do. They don't question what is handed to them; they take it. People whom I thought were my friends turned their backs on me. I know better now; in times like these, you simply find out who your real friends are. God sees all, God knows all, and in the end, it's God we answer to.

My journey into faith wasn't overnight. In fact, I was angry with God for years because I felt forsaken by him. I was blinded by anger and thought I must have done something to deserve everything that happened to me. I was afraid to get close to anyone because they might find out how damaged I was, so I spent seven years in a single life.

It wasn't until I was set up on a blind date with a man I almost didn't meet because I was afraid. He lived across the street from me and had two young children. His name was Jim, and he was a divorced police officer. There couldn't possibly be any baggage there, right? Well, something told me to meet him anyway. Our first date was a ride on his motorcycle, followed by a six-mile walk. It felt we had known each other years, even though we had just met. Jim was nine years older, a Gulf War Marine infantry veteran. I never kissed on a first date, but I did kiss him that day. We embraced. In his arms, I felt safe for the first time since I could remember. Jim became my husband on June 5th, 2007. I'm rather certain God had something to do with that little nudge. Thirteen years later, we are still each other's best friends; we never have to explain what we feel sometimes; we just get each other. We had a son born between us in 2010, and our beautiful, blended family became complete. Jim's ex-wife is even friends with me; she is a woman of God as well. We could co-parent until the stepchildren grew and had beautiful babies of their own. I had come so far, but my healing had only just begun.

I was diagnosed with papillary thyroid cancer in 2012. As far as cancers go, it's the kind you'd rather have. It's the most treatable kind with a 95% survival rate, and mine was also caught very early. That's when I knew that God is always working, protecting us. It was just enough of a wake-up call to make my healing a priority to be the best mother and wife I could be. This was also when I fell to my knees and asked God for his help. I wasn't angry with him anymore and grateful for his mercy.

It wasn't until I started to take a chance on stepping outside of my comfort zone and trying new forms of treatment such as equine therapy. That became the catalyst of my healing, probably because I was fortunate enough to have a pony growing up. I was delighted around horses as a child. However, I had always thought that chapter in my life was closed and long forgotten. There I was in Texas, thousands of miles from home and sobbing over a friendly white mule's back. From there on, I had more equine therapy closer to home. The barn owners then allowed me to volunteer there as a barn hand and treated me like family. Eventually, I got my own horse again; a stocky little Haflinger named Oggy. I jokingly call him my "mid-life crisis pony" but he has been a precious addition to our family.

I also was fortunate enough to have training in post-traumatic growth through the Warrior PATHH program. I gained a whole circle of friends and learned the concept of struggling well. They became a part of my extended family, and I finally found a new purpose- to give back and help others. My husband and I found a local church that was the perfect fit for our family, and we were welcomed there with open arms. I felt worthy of God's love and let it into my heart. I decided to let go of my anger, burdens, fears and give them all to him.

Do I still have bad days? Absolutely! I'm as mortal and fallible as the next human being. The difference is now I don't allow one bad day to convince me that I'm having a bad life.

I could have given up long ago, but no one would know my story if I did. I wouldn't have met my husband, my stepchildren, or have had my son. Those who set out to hurt me wanted to destroy my life, but why give them that satisfaction? Sometimes the best revenge is simply a life well-lived. Thanks to God, I can do just that.

My Chain Breaking Words for You:

The Samaritan woman at the well resonated with me. She was never named but her story is no less significant. The love of God and Jesus reminds that no matter how lonely we feel or how many people have betrayed us, God will never abandon us.

[10] Jesus answered and said unto her if thou knewest the gift of God, and who it is that saith to thee, give me to drink; thou wouldest have asked of him, and he would have given thee living water. -John 4-10, KJV

About Stephanie Grant

Stephanie Grant was born in Bath, Maine and raised in the midcoastal region of Maine. She joined the United States Army Reserves as a truck driver in 2000 and worked as a nursing assistant for elderly and terminally ill veterans in the civilian sector. She had thought she wanted to be a registered nurse, but her heart wasn't in it. Stephanie has a passion for writing and understanding the human condition.

In 2004, Stephanie's Army Reserve unit was called to duty to Iraq for a year long deployment. Her unit traveled throughout 10,000 miles all over Iraq, hauling everything from tanks to building materials. Stephanie and her fellow soldiers mostly faced long, hard hours on the road. Very thankfully, everyone from her unit came home even if a few had earned purple hearts within the ranks.

Stephanie decided to return to college and earned her bachelor's degree in mental health and human services from the University of Maine at Augusta. She lives in Farmingdale, Maine with her husband James and her young son. Currently, she is working on other writing projects through Michigan State University.

10

BREAKING CHAIN AFTER CHAIN

ALi Lovejoy

U.S. Air Force Veteran

Goals for this chapter:

1. Breaking the chains of family abuse

2. Challenging the perception of Autism and what it looks like in women

3. To give hope to women seeking solutions with military conflict.

Hi, I'm ALi... aka "Roper" and later on" Stevens." I joined the Air Force in 1985 to gain control of my fears and to heal after several sexual abuses throughout my adolescence. I thought joining the military would help me to be physically fit and mentally prepared to deal with aggression in any form.

Being born in the mid 60's came with a unique set of challenges. Lots of freedoms were being fought for, both on the front lines in foreign lands, as well as our cities and towns. Civil rights were at the forefront of demands, men were being drafted and women were left to fill the void. We were dealing with anger, oppression, liberation, retaliation, as soldiers were coming back from the war broken, battered and very unappreciated.

See, I was born to a woman who suffered her own abuses. First from her father and then from her first husband. She finally found the courage to leave and fell in love with my father. But before I was even born, she left him. The one thing my mom did right, was to eventually marry my adoptive dad when I was two.

Growing up I had an overabundance of challenges like special education classes. I went to vision, speech, and physical therapies, all kinds of camps and church programs. I was even sent to 6 months of etiquette school when I was 16. My parents were always saying I was oblivious to what others felt or thought, until puberty, when I became overly sensitive and very empathic.

My childhood was very hard. I could mimic adult actions, but when it came to imaginative play, forget it. I was extremely straight-forward and matter of fact. I loved puzzles and finding solutions, as I would deep dive for hours or days. Grownups found me either intriguing or very odd based on all the questions I asked.

We lived on the family homestead where my dad grew up with his uncle and grandparents. I very quickly became my dad's shadow. He was the one that taught me all the cool skills like turning wrenches, detailing cars, wiring lamps, fixing tires and farm equipment, raising and tending livestock, growing crops, and so many other useful skills. My dad is my best friend. He is my gut check and my chuckles. I do not know where I would be without him or my grandma.

It was my grandmother that taught me most of the domestic skills. She took me to cultural events as well as taught me how to polish stones, make jewelry, draw, and so much more. She really encouraged my art. I survived my youth because of these two people.

Nine months prior to joining the Air Force, I was interning at a local bank. One day I passed out and ended up hospitalized for two weeks with severe Epson Barre Syndrome (Mononucleosis). After the hospital stay, I went home to recover. I took advantage of the time and started planning my college adventure. Because of my internship I had extra credits, which allowed me to leave a couple of months early for college, if I promised to returned home for graduation to walk with my class and receive my diploma. One day after graduation my cousin came over to hang out for the day. We stopped at the park to talk to some friends. Again, not paying attention, a man followed us home. He waited till dark, broke in, and assaulted me. That left me emotionally and physically tapped. I couldn't cope on my own, I left college and I went home.

After being home for a bit my dad saw me struggling and was concerned. We talked a while and he suggested I investigate the military. I had excellent ASVAB scores, especially in mechanics, it was worth checking out. At least I would be safe. The next week my dad, grandpa and uncle, all veterans, took me down to the recruiter's office.

My grandpa insisted I go Air Force. He was a Belly Gunner on B-17's in the Army Air Core and felt I would have a better selection of career fields with opportunities to excel. It was a good thing I liked the blue uniforms!

I had a blast in basic training, a few challenges, mostly with school, but I graduated on time. The best part was during career selection, a new career opened for women, working on fighter jets. I applied and was selected, which made me one of the first women to work on jet fighters. I was so stoked! It was in tech school that I started having some intense medical issues. I was passing out, vomiting, and disoriented, with no explanation why. I went through all kinds of testing; I got counseling for the sexual assault. In the end they still had no idea what was happening, but I was still deemed worldwide deployable. A few days before I graduated, I received orders to Spain with a short temporary duty at Shaw AFB, South Carolina for advanced training on the F-16 air frame.

I was on cloud nine, I really thought I had made it. I absolutely loved my job. I was going overseas to this exotic location and getting paid to do it. Life was amazing. Until I went to out process. I got my final shots, did a UA and that's when I found out I was pregnant. Decision time. At the time there were limited facilities for pregnant women, especially overseas. So, I chose to stay stateside and go "palace front." I would transfer to a Reserve base near my hometown and do weekend training. About three months after giving birth, I collapsed and couldn't get up. I was quickly diagnosed with Gillian Barre Syndrome (GBS). Within 4 hours, I was paralyzed from the neck down. I had to be taken by Life Flight to larger hospital where I would be treated inpatient for eight weeks, then back home to do therapies and learn to live with my disability. Between the treatment and therapy, it took me about a year to fully recover.

Having gotten married six months earlier, I was eligible to reapply for active duty. It was a long shot, as the Air Force wasn't accepting prior service. But, within three months of applying, I receive a letter saying I was eligible to reenlist once I passed MEPS.

I DID IT!!! I got orders a couple weeks later to First Tactical Headquarters, Langley, VA. They changed my air frame to F-15 Eagle; bigger and more powerful. I was going to 1ˢᵗ Tac! My life was back on track.

Once I got to Langley, I was put in the dorms so I could get my schools up to date, arrange housing and childcare. After being on base about a month, I got a disturbing phone call about my husband cheating on me. After I got off the phone I was really upset and decided to go for a walk. I was sitting on a bench crying when an airman came up and asked if I was ok. I said no, and we started talking. He explained he used to be chaplain's assistant and asked if he could pray with me. We prayed, then asked if I wanted to go back to the dorms, where we could sit and talk, I said sure.

We got back to the dorms, went in, that's when he locked the door, grabbed ahold of me and started touch me. I screamed, kicked his leg, unlocked the door and ran. I couldn't believe I had just been assaulted again. I ran to a friend's room. He called our First Sergeant. After filling a report, the guy was discharged within 24 hours. As it turned out, he had done this to several other girls. I made it a priority to get off-base housing as soon as I could find a place and a roommate. Fortunately, one of the other airmen in my office was moving off base as well. I even started the divorce process.

A couple of months went by, I started having medical issues again. This time I was hospitalized with heat stroke, muscle cramps, migraines, accompanied by passing out and dizziness. I had no clue what was going on. I wasn't partying or going out to clubs, I was busy setting up a life for me and my daughter. It was at this point I was told that I had too many family issues and I needed to keep them to myself and focus solely on the military mission. That is exactly what I had been doing. My APRs were all 8's & 9's. I was in 5-level school for aircraft maintenance, working on CDCs (career field correspondence course) and I was assigned my own jet. I was so confused.

When it was time to go home to get my daughter I scheduled my leave and left as early as possible. It only took me 3 1/2 days to drive from VA to OR. I might have been a little excited. Everything went according to plan, I even finished up my divorce. Then just before my return to base, an ovarian cyst rupture & hemorrhage with yet another hospital stays. After a two-week delay, my daughter and I finally made our way back to VA.

I was fortunate to have a few good friends on base, but there was one person I couldn't wait to see: a single dad I had hung out with. We had become good friends sharing pictures and stories of our kids. We were both older than most of the people in the dorm, so we connected quickly. It turned out; he was the first person I saw on base. We chatted for a little bit, but he had an appointment, so we decided to get together later.

Soon after that we started dating, by the end of the year, we moved into a cute little beach house. Christmas was spent apart, he went to CA to see his daughter, and I was spent time with mine. While he was gone, I found out I was pregnant. It came as a shock because I was told I couldn't have anymore children. But the bigger shock came when we found we were having twins. Talk about a crazy time. I wasn't sure how this was going to turn out, but it was made clear that, I would not be doing it alone.

Being pregnant meant I went on profile, removed from all flight line activity and mobility status, and moved to a new job in the flight office. My new boss made it very clear he didn't like women in his territory. He told me "The only thing I was good for was laying on my back and spreading my legs."

Being pregnant, in a new job, and being harassed. It was at this point I found out that I was also being recommended for a mental health discharge. My new supervisor told the commander I was a troublemaker as I was manipulative and too emotional, when really I was standing up for myself and calling him out on his abuse.

I couldn't believe it; I had worked so hard to get back in. I was beyond frustrated, I was mortified. I did my best to fight it, but in the end, I went into preterm labor almost losing both my daughter and my own life to eclampsia.

The military doctor that wrote the discharge paperwork, told me to never to apply for benefits he made sure I would never see a dime, that he tried everything up in a nice neat little package. His diagnoses for me a" personality and dissociative disorder." That diagnosis did more than stop my benefits, it caused employment issues, doctors' issues, wrong medications which almost killed me several times, and mistreatment from medical personnel.

My case was not straight forward. Some of the things that affected me had no diagnosis at the time. However, that didn't mean there was nothing wrong or that military service didn't cause life altering damage. It has only been the last 7 years that we have been able to put the whole picture together, getting the correct diagnosis.

It took me over 20 years to rectify the issues. Thankfully, my military medical and personnel records had everything I needed to get the correct diagnosis, they just needed to be read in context. I am happy to say that as of today, I receive an enormous amount of counseling and am not just surviving - I am thriving. In the end I am here to bring hope!

Today we now know that the vomiting and passing out was from a cardiac condition known as Post Ossicular Tachycardia Syndrome (POTS) that causes autonomic nervous system disfunction. I have a rare form which raise and rapidly lowers my blood pressure when sitting, standing, walking, or exercising. This is directly linked to the Epson Barre Syndrome. The connection was unknown at the time but confirmed today.

Today we also know that I have extreme Mast Cell Activation disorder

(MACD) that causes significant symptoms from internal inflammation. Everything from stroke symptoms to anaphylaxis, when activated. I was exposed to harsh chemicals both fixing and cleaning the jets causing migraine headaches, internal swelling of the brain, lungs and heart, again directly related.

We know that my paralysis was caused by immunizations combined with extreme fatigue due to environmental conditions and physical conditioning. It is the next stage of autonomic dysfunction. This virus sits dormmate in the spinal column and when presented with extreme conditions, activates, starting the process of paralysis. Beginning at the feet, working up the legs slowly weakening them, then moving rapidly through the trunk of the body, up the spine, into the arms, up through the neck to the head. The weaker the body gets the more it loses its ability to not only move, but the nerves begin to go crazy. Next the lungs shut down and if left untreated, death. I am fortunate to have survived with how little they knew about it back in the 1980's. It is still rare, but thanks to the Covid 19 shots, most people have heard of it.

The Military Sexual Trauma (MST) and complex trauma (C-PTSD), that I suffered has been heard and validated. Not only did it affect my employment opportunities and security clearances, but it also affected my personal life. I was 50 years old when they figured out, I was on the Autism Spectrum. I think in pictures and communicate by mimicking. I learn by doing and seeing. Even though I have a very high IQ, words are confusing as they mean many things. I am very good at what the mental health community calls "masking." Life was a struggle for many years, but it is so much easier when you have the right diagnosis.

Today I am artist, designer, author, public speaker, and philanthropist who owns her own business, focusing on art and helping others. I live on top of a mountain with my family and two dogs. Oh, and you know that single father I was dating, well we have been happily married now for over three decades, with 4 biological & 6 adopted children, and 29 grandchildren. Life is nothing short of amazing!!!

My Chain Breaking Words for You:

Never stop moving forward and seeking the truth. Like I found out just because there were no relivant answers at the time doesn't mean the answers didn't exist. So what do you need to move forward?

About ALi Lovejoy

ALi… a brand that turned into her name. A professional photographer (ali.AnnetteLovejoyimagery.com), veteran, designer, facilitator, public speaker, philanthropist and now contributing author for Veterans Unchained Women's Anthology.

After years of struggling with severe medical issues and feeling abandoned by the military who mis-diagnosed her with a misleading psychiatric condition. ALi… took matters into her own hands and sought realistic answers. Between her military records, veterans service officer and longtime doctors, it was found that many of ALi's… issues were due to being the autism spectrum not a psychiatric condition.

Now ALi… is breaking the chain of long-time abuse and living her dream. She lives on top of a mountain, making jewelry and producing art to sell. Active in her local community, ALi… enjoys teaching and education people on various aspects of health & wellness as well as veterans' issues. ALi… also really loves helping others through her philanthropy program which gives scholarships, internships, financial assistance, and emergency funds to those in need. You can find more information on her website InspiringALisHeart.org

11

AS THE SWEAT DRIPS

Juanita A. Terry-Wentz

U.S. Army Veteran

The heater has finally warmed up most of the mats on the floor and it's turning off now. It's been about 45 minutes since I switched on the heat. My body is warm and stretched. This is "me" time. No one else. My time! I am selfish about my time! I deserve my time! It's my healing time. I'm a "work in progress," as I pray, heal, grow, learn about me and things of this world. My warmup partner is a 120 lb. heavy bag that hangs along south wall of our Dojo. My bag is referred to as Marilyn because this bag is indented in the middle from the workouts, which gives the bag an hourglass look. As I am gearing down and getting ready for Kata, I reflect on why I ever started training in Martial Arts. Why would I go through all of this pain to train? I look at the wall of mirrors. I see a different body from when I started this journey. But wait... I still think the same. Angry, hurt, don't trust, want revenge, dwell on hate and what I would do.

My mind wanders off. This time it's to me standing at the doorstep. Waiting for that door to open. To see that face. To be in that moment. To face my fear of him. To see that look as I strike him repeatedly. To see that fear. That fear... his fear... in his eyes. I get stuck in that moment in my mind. No control. My mind seeks vengeance. I need to be in control. My body is shaking now, throat starts closing, there's pressure on my chest, my body is on fire, I have an uncontrollable need to go, leave, run, get away! Get away now! My heart is racing. I can't... function! Reach! I'm screaming inside, Reach out! I reach out for the cold brick walls, with uneven texture. I run my fingers across them repeatedly, as I walk back and forth, saying I am ok, I am safe, I am ok, I am safe. Tears fill my eyes as I choke out these words. I see that it's one of those days. And the day has just begun. I no longer stress about what time I wake up.

It's life for now, work through it and with it. It's what happens when I have fought in my sleep. Or dwelled on a moment from the day before. I begin to walk in the infinity pattern on the mats and I count 1,2, 3, A, B, C, 4, 5, 6, D, E, F, as I focus on my breath. Deep breaths, that's it. Take another one. And another. I get lost in my count as each breath gets slower and the body starts to relax. I start my count over and over. My pace slows and I feel myself coming back to reality. I am here. I am now. I am ok.

I feel the cold sweat dripping down the back of my arms, and there's this little chill across the upper part of my body that follows. I can hear the crackling flame of the heater in the background as it works hard to warm the air and eventually the matts on the floor. As I look around this large room with white brick walls, I thank God for this place. We were blessed with the opportunity to give back, and that was all that was needed. We found a building with a storage room next to the main large room, big enough to live in. This is our new live-in Dojo! Out in the middle of nowhere. An almost forgotten old mining ghost town, across from the famous Clown Motel in Tonopah, Nevada. With the bright white walls everywhere, we put 5-foot-tall mirrors across the east wall of the large room. There are bold red and black stripes that run along the top of the wall and a black stripe at the base. 117 each, 44-inch square,1 5/8-inch-thick red and black training mats covering 70% of the training floor. There are four 120 lb. hanging heavy bags that drape to the floor along the south wall and a weight training area along the north wall. As I walk across the matts, and I'm peeling off the boxing gloves. I can feel the warmth a little softness under my feet. And yet still others are cold and firm where the heat has not reached. The sound of the boxing gloves velcro is so loud. Ugh… No matter how quiet you try to be. Lol. I set them down by the mirrors. I remove the shin guards that kept sliding around from sweat dripping legs. It's so annoying at times to have to stop to move them back to where they belong. That's what I get for not wearing a rash guard. I chastise myself for thinking it would be a different outcome. I chime out, "drink water!" A healthy distraction from the task on hand. Finding a warm spot on the mats, I begin stretching my buttocks and lower back. Looks like I need to add some CBD crème on my aching parts. "Drink water!" I'm stalling. Why am I stalling? Get to it! You have to. You need to. People are watching you and they see the outside of you has changed. You need to keep going. Your kids look up to you. Your common-law husband talks highly of you. Your momma and dad worry and are proud of your accomplishments. I see what the inside of me is forming into. Not happy, angry with how a thought can run through you and affect you in such away. That alters your perception of reality.

The changes from within; it is a fight from within. "Maintain," I say. This is real and this is now. I fight to be in control of my feelings, my thoughts, my actions, my surroundings. Stretch and clear your mind of ill thoughts. Clear your mind of blood. Clear your mind of furry. Clear your mind… breathe… Lord God, give me strength. I need some comfort, Lord. I close my eyes and breathe. A warm flush runs over my body. I smile and say, "Thank you, God." I know that was you, Lord. With eyes wide open and looking past the white walls, I tell myself I can dothis. Rubbing CBD crème on my right-side groin, hips, buttocks, lower back and knees. Oh yes! That's it. Ahhhh….thank goodness for the crème. It helps tremendously with pain management. I don't know how in the world I ever lived without this crème. I follow up with a couple hits of wax. Takes a few minutes for those meds to kick in and I can move with minimal pain. I wanna punch the doctor that took three x-rays and said, "You're not broken or bleeding. Go back to work. Every time I respond with" M…F…" I'm telling you; something is wrong with my groin area. This is too much pain. Ugh… don't go there brain. Focus on the task at hand. It didn't do any good to complain and seek treatment then and it's not changed now. Time spent doing my physical sessions have changed my body. But the mind, the mind has a different task that is hindered with a blockage. And I can't see it. I know it's there. Every day is a battle. Every day I commit time for my mind to catch up with my body. I face the mirrored wall. Clear your mind, I say. It's time to train. I begin to move slowly from one stance to another. There's so much time for the mind to wander. Don't do that. Stay here and work your Kata. Move onto a few more stances. I repeat the movements and I cringe at times and wobble on unsteady knees. Pain runs through the body. Stand fast. Hold. Don't give in to the pain. Push past this. You are 54 years old, you raised 4 kids that are all grown and holding their own. You got this! Keep going!

Where did the time go? Why did time go this way? When will this be over? I need to be strong. They are still watching. They are always watching. Another time in my life seeps into my mind. Flashes of my oldest daughter fill my thoughts. The young little beautiful big-eyed baby, all neatly braided hair. In a cute white pressed Ninja Turtles T-shirt and shorts. Her creamy soft dark brown skin shining in the sun. That look she has with those big brown eyes. The innocence… innocence lost. Pain endured. I can smell it. I can feel it.

Shake it off!!! Shake it off!!! Move from that space! Physically and mentally! Move!!! Reach for something solid that is next to you. I hear screams inside of me. I feel the screams inside of me. What? Wait? No!!! No!!! No!!! I run through some movements fast and hard. I do it again and again. Ah… the feel of destroying what is haunting you. I catch a mistake in my movements, and I slow down and do it again. I look at my stances in the wall of mirrors. My focus has been redirected and I am in training mode. Thank you, God. Thank you…

Time goes by and I am interrupted by my hubby. He says it's time to take a break now and get something to eat. I smile and nod ok. I turn to the wall of mirrors, bow and remove my belt and GI top. As I bend over to place my belt next to my gloves, the drips of sweat from my brow, lands on the matts below. I look around room and say, "Thank you, God, for another day on this earth. Thank you, God, for being the comfort that is needed. Thank you, God, for giving me strength to regain my thoughts, of my perception of self-control." Through all the wrong doings and happenings in my life from as early as I can remember in a foster home, up to the day I stood my ground from an abusive husband. Always fighting to be me, to be strong, to be in control of an uncontrollable life. Fighting for what is right! Fighting to protect those who cannot protect themselves. You, God. You. You have always been there for me.

All I need to do is ask…

My Chain Breaking Words for You:

Change is Inevitable... Growth is Optional...

About Juanita A. Terry-Wentz

I'm still here... I'm still breathing. I am a no-nonsense, short-fused, serious individual with artistic and mechanical abilities, that depends on my relationship with GOD and JESUS. My heart cries out for the less fortunate and reaches out when the heart says so. Broken physically and mentally from years of abuse and neglect, regretfully took its toll on loving life. Until that day... that day in time. It's those moments in time that change your "forever." I started my martial arts journey at the *Krazy* age of 49. I have been "The Reluctant Black Belt" from day one. Lol... At times, even I need to look back at where I've been. Here, is the perfect avenue to do so.

12

HOPE DEFERRED TO HOPE RESTORED

Gloria Nesloney

U.S. Marine Corps Veteran

Tears flooded my eyes when I could not see past the pain so many years ago. I am taken back to the time when wordy prayers seemed endless and aimless. I didn't have real requests or supplications, only complaints and sadness. It all started while I was assigned to my duty station in 1993. I requested liberty the weekend of the Valentine's. It was a common practice to request leave in advance so that your duties were completed, or someone could be placed in position to fill in. A couple of others requested liberty on the same weekend. Our names were placed on a roster so everyone could see who was going to be out and who was staying to help with duties.

I saved some money to take a taxi to visit several locations outside the base. I had plans to eat a fancy lunch, go sightseeing, go shopping and finally spend the night off-base for the first time. I was captivated by the dew drops that lingered to collect under the leaves and then drip slowly to the ground. My moment of solace and quietness kept me at the forest long enough to stay before the evening hours.

As it started getting dark, I asked my taxi driver to take me to the mall. I stayed about three hours until the stores were beginning to close. As I was waiting for my taxi ride, I saw some of my platoon. They asked where I was staying. I didn't tell anyone because I didn't want any company. So, I told them I was going to continue to sight see different areas around town. They waved goodbye and we parted our ways.

Later that evening I had checked into a hotel that most of the comrades mentioned because the rates were low, and they had military discounts. The evening went well, and I was looking forward to some quiet rest. However, that night, I had a nightmare; at least I thought it was a nightmare, until I woke up. When I woke up I had a massive headache unlike a regular migraine. I woke up in a bathtub that was running with water with a trail of blood. I had a gash on the back of my head and blood was dried to my hair. I had a head injury.

Oddly, I had no clothes on and the bathtub was overflowing. The trickling of water drops can be heard. How the heck did I hit my head?

Why didn't I have clothes on? Why was I in the bathtub? Why was the water overflowing? I stepped out of the bathroom to find something to wear. I found my clothes nicely folded and set on a chair in the bedroom. I don't remember taking my clothes off. I had always slept with clothes on in case of an emergency. I also would not have showered until the morning. I was not a bath person. I am a very routine person. So, yes, I was confused.

When I fixed myself up and was ready to leave the hotel, the door was unlocked. That was when I realized something happened and the memory started coming. I never would have known that the nightmare was actually happening to me, physically. In the nightmare, a figure is opening my door; I remembered his face, his words, his last name, his cologne of Cool Water. I left scratches on his face and on his chest. In the nightmare, the perpetrator knocked me behind my head while he was raping me. He was from my platoon.

I told the hotel personnel about the incident, but they said it was a military issue and needed to be dealt with by the military. I was well enough to call a taxi from the front desk. I signed back in on the roster and I went to my Staff Sergeant to report the incident. When I pointed to the individual's name that was on the roster, I was told to leave the office or I would be reprimanded for slandering. I went back to the barracks, and I was furious. I knew I was going to have to face the platoon Monday morning.

Before I was able to go to bed that evening, I was escorted by two Military Police. I was transported along with another female from my platoon. We were admitted to a hospital for evaluation and a rape kit was provided for us. I had never heard of a rape kit, or a pregnancy prevention shot that was administered to both of us. We were interrogated. It was a terrible experience. We were sent back to the barracks and instructed not to speak to each other or speak to anyone about what happened. Early Monday morning, I stood in front of my Commanding Officer and the Administrative Committee who was going to determine my future in the military. I was treated like the villain instead of like the victim. The Staff Sergeant of my platoon just stood there watching me try to keep my bearing while I wished he would read my mind that was screaming inside, "TELL THEM THE TRUTH."

That was the day I determined that I would tell the truth instead of being loyal. See in the military there is a code of conduct, and nowhere does it say to be honest, it says to be loyal. No one was loyal to me the day I needed them to have my back, be on my side, and fight for me. I later found out that the individual who broke into my hotel room was not his first time to rape; I could only pray it would have been his last.

I had shame, guilt, and no will to live. I wanted to make my parents proud of me, but they couldn't know the truth about me being raped, so I overdosed in a suicide attempt. Time was of the essence if I was going to survive, but no one knew how long I was out when I was found unconscious. No one knew why a seemingly happy young successful lady would want to hurt themselves. If anyone knew, it would be the Commanding Officer, the Administrative Committee, and my platoon Staff Sergeant.

You may have heard of people having an out of body experience, seeing the light, seeing heaven, seeing their bodies on the hospital bed. I didn't believe those kinds of stories either until it happened to me. It happened the day I died on April 7, 1993. However, I didn't see light or heaven. I could not speak, but I could yell. However, no one could hear me. I saw myself from above my body; I could see the shadows of doctors working on me. I felt my body leave the ceiling and go to a dreary place where I saw sheer terror. It was like a battleground with souls scratching the walls as if trying to get out of a burning pit. I was in complete darkness, but I could still see glimpses of those who seemed to be screaming but I couldn't help them. I feared as I have never feared before. I had an encounter with death and visited hell. Though brief, it was enough to know that was not where I wanted to be.

What was supposed to be my career of military life was a crushed dream. My identity was labeled as TBI, MST, MPD, and PTSD. I no longer felt like a mighty warrior, so I didn't believe it anymore. I shut down from anything called life and found myself at psychiatric appointments that only tried to treat my symptoms instead of the real issues. I was raped, I was hurt, I was angry, I did not trust people, and I hated my life.

I learned how to be cold, bitter, and act out in bouts of rage. I learned to push people away. I would put on my stern, get out of my face, look, and did not let people get close to me. From my military training, I learned how to fuel the fire that raged inside of me. I was going to be a mean green fighting machine. I had bottled up my emotions; eventually, they blew up like a volcano, an inferno that seemed inescapable. Sometimes I would be venomous towards those who cared for me or tried to help me. I had secrets I hid, I learned how to live a double life, and I learned how to harbor hatred in my heart. The spiral of life was only getting deeper, darker, and more dreadful. All those emotions exploded back in my face when I tried to live my reality without God, Jesus, or Holy Spirit.

On Labor Day of September 1995, I was sitting under the canopy of a shaded atrium and the smell of jasmine was in the air when I looked up at the trees above. Again, I saw a small beam of light reflecting the dew under the leaf. I was taken back to all the other times I had seen this and the terrible triggers it brought. The Lord spoke to me and said, "Gloria, I will replace old memories with new ones." So I prayed. There are still some things I don't remember well from my past, but I can recall the miracles the Lord has done since. What really caught me off guard is that the Lord knows my name.

That day I fell. I fell hard. I fell hard in love. I fell hard in love with Jesus. For the first time, I asked Jesus to come into my heart. I needed a change in my life, and thankfully, Jesus was the answer I was looking for. There were still the issues of the heart that the Lord wanted to heal. One day the Lord asked me, "Gloria, will you allow me to love you?"

Right away, I answered, "Yes, Lord, I will allow you to love me." Then he asked me another question. "Gloria, will you allow Me to love you through someone else?" I came undone. I said, "Lord, you know I don't trust anyone with my heart but You. No man has ever given me a reason to believe in love. You're going to have to help me with this, but Yes, Lord I trust you. I will allow you to love me through someone else." The Lord gave me a new memory, a memory of celebration when I was proposed to on Valentine's Day in 2014 at the age of 40. My heart was healed; my answer was "Yes." I couldn't believe how safe I felt for the very first time with a man ever.

I have been given a second chance through the grace and love of God. I have found the purpose through pain. My identity is not what I have gone through or what others have labeled me through the issues I went through. My identity is in Jesus and what He has done in me. Tears of joy flood my eyes now that I can see past the pain. The terrible memories are fewer and farther between. I am taken back now to when prayers were answered, miracles have occurred, and I have been set free from the torment. I have found my reason to live. I help others through inner healing from traumatic events. I found the answer to overcome the casualties in my mind was through the power of prayer, the gift of the Holy Spirit, and salvation through Jesus. I learned how to lean on Jesus when I was scared, felt alone, or needed to cry on someone's shoulder. I learned that what I have gone through is going to help others find hope in life, in their future, and in God.

My Chain Breaking Words for You:

The secrets I hid and the despair I felt surmounted the existence to want to live. But God had plans for me. He had a future for me that I could not yet see. He is using my victory to help women overcome challenges after trauma. Jeremiah 29:11

About Gloria Nesloney

Gloria Nesloney has been serving the Lord since 1995 experiencing personal transformation and revival. She was called into ministry in 1998 and ministered in garages, street corners, and different denominations in South Texas. She studied through the International School of Ministry, Commission to Every Nation Missionary Program, and God's Living Word Ministry as a licensed minister and has received a Doctorate of Divinity. She is a student at Hillsdale College and Christian Leaders Institute / Alliance for continued education.

Light For Every Nation - International Christian Networking Ministry was birthed in January 2000 as a corridor for ministers and ministries. Through Light for Every Nation, Gloria serves as a free webpage host to grow ministries and provide Christian resources. Since 2002, she has conducted evangelical, medical, and missionary ministry in Texas, Mexico, Guatemala, Panama, and Uganda. In June 2021, Gloria commenced an online group called S.T.E.P. UP - WFWS as a monthly challenge for women faith walkers and seekers to grow in relationship with God, Jesus, and Holy Spirit.

As a United States Marine Corps Veteran, Gloria attends to Women Veterans who need inner healing from traumatic events. She volunteers to help the wounded woman warrior find hope. She counsels those who are in or overcoming addictions and help families who need restoration. Serving at rescue homes and shelters has helped her engage women who are in transition from prison, or destructive lifestyles, to a life in Christ with a new hope and focus on freedom.

Her interests are spiritual warfare and victories through prayer and fasting, deliverance, healing, and the testimonies that only come from the manifold gifts of the Holy Spirit.

Gloria and her husband, Malcolm, are surrounded by spiritual fathers and mothers, mentors, teachers, and pastoral friends they stay in contact with on a day-to-day basis. They are accountable to those who watch over them and encourage each person to do the same. She and her husband currently serve the ecuministry and ecclesia in the Coastal Bend District in South Texas.

Books by Gloria Nesloney

From Glory To Glory: Enraptured

From Glory To Glory: The Dew Under The Leaf

From Glory To Glory: In His Time

Contact Information

Website and Blog: www.lightforeverynation.com

Email: lightforeverynation@yahoo.com

Online Ministry Group: S.T.E.P. UP - WFWS

13

IT'S GOOD ENOUGH

Dr. Patricia M. Roebuck

U.S. Navy Veteran

I made Master Chief in 18 years, in a time when that was not an everyday occurrence, especially as a female Sailor. I am on a recruiting tour in a West Texas town as the Recruiter in Charge. I am sitting in my office listening to one of my recruiters recount an applicant's "home" visit. I place home in quotes as it is only that by definition - the place where one lives permanently as a member of a family or household - not by the "home is where the heart is" standard. The applicant is a young male from an impoverished home about to graduate high school and has no viable opportunities other than the local discount store. As the young applicant is not yet 18, we must get his mother's consent and written approval. The recruiter describes the run-down apartment in the wrong part of town and the squalor environment in which this applicant lives. The mother is not happy with this intrusion and looks straight at the recruiter and states, "I will break both his legs before he leaves me. Welfare's good enough for me; it's good enough for him."

Bam! I am my younger self, standing in one of a string of unpleasant "homes" hearing my mother tell me, "Why do you think you deserve any better? It's good enough."

I am jolted back to the office as my recruiter sighs out an expressive and loud, "Wow!" Wow indeed. It was easy for the recruiter to sit there with an astonished look thinking of the nonsensicalness of this mother's words. We know what a great opportunity this would be for the applicant and his family; I know how the Navy became my refuge from a storm. I look supportively at the recruiter and explain that the young man will have to make the decision on his own and close out the file.

I am carried back to the day I told my mom that I had joined the Navy and would be leaving in two days. She looked at me and asked one question and made a bitter statement, as only she could. I slowly weave my way back to the present, and I am reminded again of the foundation of nurturing that I was raised on, "it's good enough." There is no need to dream or want more in life; I was not capable, nor did I deserve better - it's good enough.

My upbringing was one of poverty, mental and physical abuse, disregard and isolation, and mockery and scorn. This is all from an absent father and a bitter mother whose divorce was the best thing they ever did as parents for their four children. My father was a tyrannical and arrogant man. We were his shame and embarrassment. My mother was a vicious and inattentive woman raised in mental and physical abuse, further wounded by my father. We were her cross to bear; the problems she could not escape.

This is a familiar story, especially in the 1970s – man and woman divorce, woman left to raise children, children survive. However, the difference in this story is the constant barrage of insults, threats, oppression, exploitation, neglect, and actions that molded the children into dwellers of a world that's good enough. The children became their own islands in a pool of sharks, and lest they become fodder, were taught to add to the cruelty on the others that were being targeted. If the attack was on someone else, it was not on you.

My father was a hard man. I can honestly say I do not remember getting any type of affection from this man - ever. I remember him sticking his foot out to trip me and laughing at my sprawled-out body on the floor. Or the time he did not like what I was saying, so he pushed my face into my dinner plate. The stretches of time my brother and I would have to sit with liquid dish soap sliding up and down our tongues because of some slight we had hurled his way. The times he beat our mother or brother as he mostly left the emotional abuse for the three girls – only a slap or smack, here and there when he could be bothered.

The constant fog of foreboding dread and anxiety filled the house when he was around, always walking on eggshells in case we wake the beast. He was a man that could turn a phrase, such as the classic parent expression, "Stop crying, or I'll give you something to cry about." But his repertoire of insults and threats begot many awful phrases such as "Shut up, or I'll rip your head off and shit down your windpipe," or "If you don't stop, I will rip your arms off and beat you with the bloody stumps," said to children. The offenses grew as we did to more adult content, which I will not repeat. When my parents finally divorced, we were ostracized from his side of the family and isolated. We were left with a very bitter woman, vulnerable and ill-prepared to care for herself, let alone four children.

My mother was an acrimonious woman; bouts of depression, anger, and a woeful demeanor to life did not make for a loving environment. Life, or as she would say, God, had forsaken her. She was quick with a slap, spanking, or a vile comment, and each of her children received their very own catalog of insults and abuses. I can only speak to mine, ranging from the vanilla insult such as, "Why do you think you deserve more? You are not that good?" to more scathing insults such as, "You are so lucky abortions were not legal." "I refused to accept my pregnancy with you until your birth," "When you were born, the lightbulb blew out, and the room was dark; you continue to bring dark with you," "You are such a little bitch," all said to a child. These are just a few of the taunts she repeated throughout the entirety of her life at me, literally to her bitter end.

She was not only venomous with her constant barrage of insults, but she would manipulate the others to rally around her and insult or physically attack each other for her amusement. I did not realize that siblings did not perform "cage fights" with each other until I was older. Moreover, she was never one to encourage us in case we did not get chosen or failed. She would simply tell us that we were not good enough; she did not want to be bothered by our tears and disappointment. Yes, her words. Also, she was the queen of the back-handed compliment. She would say, "I did not have an ugly child, but you are by far the ugliest child I have." "If you would lose 20lbs, you would only be a heifer," and more. When my younger sister and I talk about these things, my sister believes it was the best she could do. I do not believe that; I think it was the best she cared to do.

Fast-forward, and I am in my second year of college, working two jobs and still living in a three-bed, one bath apartment with my mother, two sisters, and brother. I am having a hard time in school, and half my paychecks go to my mother. I am 19 and still sleeping in a full bed with my 21-year-old sister, living in unpleasant conditions suffering constant badgering from my mother that I am wasting my time with school and should get a full-time job. I am at a point where I know if I do not do something drastic, I will be stuck living like this forever. If I do not do something, I will be a welfare mom, stuck in an unfulfilled life of regret and resentment. I decided that I would join the Air Force (they had cuter uniforms) for four years, get some money for college, and try again on my own.

It was a Monday, and I went to the recruiting offices downtown; all four services worked out of the same offices. I walked into the loft and marched over to the Air Force office, avoiding the other services. This guy never took his feet off the desk as he informed me that they were not recruiting any women at that time. Seriously, he never took his feet off the desk. I was not even good enough for military service. Dejected, I walked out of the office only to be blocked by a taller Filipino man in a khaki uniform. His name was Max Factor (yes, Max Factor), and he was a Chief, and he could help me. And he did.

It is Tuesday, and I passed all the physical and mental exams as I spent the entire day at MEPS, the Military Enlisted Processing Station. I am classified as Cryptologic (Collection) Technician (CTR) and told I would fly out on Thursday to Orlando, Florida, for boot camp. I quit both my jobs and went home to tell my family.

It is Wednesday, I must report to a hotel next to the airport so that they are sure that I will get on the plane. My mother took me to the hotel, where she looked at me and asked one question, "Well, who is going to do all the cleaning now?" and made a bitter statement, "No worry, you'll be back in a week; they won't want you after that."

It is Thursday, I am sitting on a plane, ready to take my first plane ride to a different world. I still believe that I am not good enough, but I did learn this from school. In the 1970s, Harvard professor Laurel Thatcher Ulrich coined the phrase, "Well-behaved women seldom make history." I did not think I would make history; however, I knew at that moment I was changing mine. Thirty years later, I retired as a group Master Chief, the Command Master Chief for an Admiral. Me, the girl that was not good enough.

That 30 years in the Navy taught me so much, beginning with my turn in boot camp. I had to learn not to smile as I was being "dressed down" by the Company Commander for some indiscretion I had committed. I always thought to myself, "This is nothing; I've been abused by better." I would smile, thanking my parents for helping me forge the invisible steel armor I wore, which carried me through my "A" and "C" Schools. However, no matter how hard I worked or how much I exceeded requirements, I was always just short of being chosen for a leadership position, meritorious promotion, or even a simple "atta boy." Obviously, I was not good enough; I would try harder.

Off to my first duty station, and again I am treated strangely, like I shouldn't be there. During one of my first Quarters, a Senior Chief noticed a discrepancy on my uniform and started poking my chest. Tears of frustration dropped from my eye, and the tirade of "Why girls did not belong in the service" lasted until we were excused. I went to the head, looked in the mirror, and realized that while I may not be good enough on that day, no one would ever see me cry again.

Things changed for me after that. I found great mentors; truth be told, they found me. They knew that while I did not need to be handled with kid gloves, they saw potential. They pushed me, challenged me, taught me, and admonished me when required. I learned to compartmentalize, take the negative and learn from it, and that fair was not an adult word. I was held back only by my own insecurities, biases, and predispositions. I was allowed to discover who I was through hardships, successes, extra duty, taking the tough assignments, but always mindful of bringing as many of the misfit toys along with me.

I became a leader, a coach, a mentor. I was selected to the ranks of Chief, Senior Chief, Master Chief, and Command Master Chief and worked for and with some of the greatest Sailors the Navy had to offer. I lead on land, at sea, and "boots on ground" in awe of the sheer virtuosity and skill of my Sailors. I accomplished many "Firsts" in the Navy, and some would call me a trailblazer. I was part of the original "Women at Sea" program that introduced women onto combatants and subsequently detailed to ship's company on a Spruance class destroyer. I was the first female country CMC for Kuwait during OEF/OIF, "boots on ground." I was the first female Group Master Chief at Surface Group Middle Pacific, Hawaii. I was proud of everything I had accomplished. And yes, I was told by some that I was not good enough. However, I know I was a good Sailor, Shipmate, and Chief. No, I was a great Sailor, Shipmate, and Master Chief!

I have been retired for seven years and what does an old pirate do when she is retired? She gets a lot of counseling to address not only her childhood trauma, but also her PTSD. She goes to school and finishes her undergraduate, three master's programs, and a doctorate in management. She starts teaching in an MBA program and decides she needs a doctorate in education, because she feels she is still not good enough. She becomes the caretaker of her father's ashes at his death (he did die alone) and was her mother's caretaker until she died in her home. My mother, beating me and screaming that she hated me, to the very end of her life.

I always live in a state of insignificance, "I am unworthy of praise. I am unworthy of success. I could have done more. I should have done more. What else could be lurking around the corner?" My mind is full of self-sabotaging thoughts placed there by my childhood past and adult distress. Not to say that there were not good times; however, there were many incidents that forged a path of low self-esteem and muted confidence. These walls that have been built can be difficult to climb at times, but I am very conscious of how I acknowledge them when they "creep" into my mind. I continue my self-reflection hoping to find a way to give myself the Grace – the Grace to know that I am good enough.

My Chain Breaking Words for You:

There comes a point when you have to realize that you will never be good enough for some people. The question is, is that their problem or yours?

May you live long enough to know why you were born.

~ Cherokee Birth Wish ~

About Dr. Patricia M. Roebuck

Patricia Roebuck is a 30-year Navy veteran. She served at various duty stations including four overseas tours, two sea tours onboard the USS KINKAID (DD-965) and USS CHAFEE (DDG-90) and direct support onboard the USS BLUE RIDGE (LCC-19), USS GERMANTOWN (LSD-42), and USS BELLEAU WOOD (LHA-3) as part of the "Women at Sea" program, has five Command Master Chief Tours, to include a tour in Kuwait as the Kuwait Country CMC for United States Naval Forces Central Command (NAVCENT) during Operation Enduring Freedom, and the Group Master Chief or Commander Naval Surface Group, Middle Pacific. She was born in Port Hueneme, CA and was raised in South San Diego, CA but calls Texas her home. She has six adult children and lives in Montgomery, TX with her husband Chris, who is also a 30-year Navy veteran. She enjoys sewing and quilting in her spare time when she is not teaching and learning working on her second doctorate.

14

UNDELIVERABLE LOVE

TaMara Sewell-Craig

U.S. Army Veteran

The Assignment

When you hear the word assignment what comes to mind? What pops into my mind is school. The Webster Dictionary definition of the term *"assignment"* is a noun in which means a person, place or thing. The definitive meaning is a task or piece of work assigned to someone as a part of a job or course of study or the attribution of someone or something as belonging.

As I sit here, approximately 3 months post-divorce, I began to try to look at the marriage in a positive perspective. I began to ask myself, "What was I supposed to learn from this almost 10-year marriage?" The Lord spoke to me loud and clear and said I placed you *on assignment*. That struck me as odd, since I loved this man and had children by him and now, I was supposed to look at him like a science project or an English paper? Well, I started to dissect the lessons I learned while in the marriage and after the marriage.

Getting a lot off my chest seems to be my story lately. For years, I have been holding traumatic life instances in by pushing them to the back of my mind as if they never happened. However, we all know that those traumatic instances always manifest at the most inopportune moments. As I sit here thinking about my future, I am daydreaming about where I would like to be in five and even ten years from now. In ten years, I will be 50 years old! WOW! My wish for my children and myself is for us to be living in our own home that I plan to purchase within the next three or so years. In addition, I plan to have a husband who cherishes and loves me for who I am and not for what I can do for them. You see, one thing I know for sure is that I am a giver and a people pleaser.

Giving is second nature to me. I live to give, and the universe ALWAYS sees me through; no matter how I might feel or how little I believe. The universe and the love given to me is always right on time. As far as being a giver, I certainly believe that you must be equally yoked. Therefore, my life partner/husband will be a person who can pour life back into me, as I will do to him. In other words, he cannot be a taker. Being in a marriage with a taker, literally takes a toll on your mind, body, and soul. As this point in my life, I have nothing left to give him. My husband of 8 years (dated for 5 years off and on prior) is a take, take, taker. He has depleted me.

As I think about it, Ethan kicked and screamed about being married. For the five years we dated, he kept saying he did not date and he did not want a relationship. However, we did everything together from the day we met, to the day we got engaged to be married. He allowed me to have his second line on his phone bill, gave me a washer and dryer for my apartment. He funded me when I needed help, and we spent quality time together. A lot of quality time. In hindsight, that was "love bombing" and now I can easily recognize that behavior from a mile away. While we were in our first year of dating, I was in a relationship all by myself. I wanted out but I still stayed. I stayed because I wanted real love.

He was my rock in this world I was transitioning in from the military to civilian life. I wanted so badly to be the support he was to me; however, his pride would not allow me to be there for him in any way other than money. He told me not to shop for him, he did his own laundry, I would text him to be safe on the road at night and he would not respond. I would send him pictures of me, and he would not respond. I could not get him to deposit anything into me. I had to start asking him, did you get the pics or text I sent you?

No reciprocation from your partner is considered emotional abuse.

"Any act including confinement, isolation, verbal assault, humiliation, intimidation, infantilization, or any other treatment which may diminish the sense of identity, dignity, and self-worth." (Tracy, 2012).

Losing oneself in a marriage uncommonly mentioned when the thrill is gone, or the rose is off the bloom. No one tells you about the dark side of marriage. The moments when you go a long with your spouse so much that you forget what you genuinely want for yourself. He does not ask you about your dreams nor does he include you in his. No one talks about once you have children; it is imperative to keep your marriage alive, but it must be two-fold. You cannot pour into a marriage with a hole at the bottom of the bucket. Your requests are denied, your opinions do not matter, and when you get angry, no one cares. You just simply sweep things under a rug and close the door. That is, until you open the closet, and all of the skeletons fall out.

Skeletons are the outer shell of a (in this case) human body. That is how I felt once I made the choice to go to counseling because I had known for a very long time that I displayed communication issues. When I met Ethan, he helped me come out of my shell and taught me how not to hold things in regarding our relationship. I could not bring up anything that happened in the past if I did not say anything at that specific time and only at that time. Therefore, that stuck with me throughout our marriage. The counseling that I began seeking started to bring out issues that we unresolved prior to us having our children.

Once I began to explain to Ethan, why these issues were coming up because of counseling. He did not want to discuss and of the issues, did not want to come to any sessions, nor did he want to provide the closure I needed to move on. Ethan cheated on me and the girl was cute. The way he posed in the pictures on social media is the way that he should have been with me. He was not kissing me the way he actually posed for those pictures. Nor did he ever come behind me affectionately and hug me as he was posed in the picture.

Therefore, I stayed. I did not leave. He threatened me not to talk to the girl even though she was persistent. She contacted me on Facebook with a profile picture of him and her. I was completely shocked and hurt. Once I confronted him, he was angry! I can only assume that he was angry because he was caught. You should have seen his face. You would have thought he had seen a ghost! He had the nerve to even throw a pillow at me but missed.

For the life of me, I could not understand why he was angry with me. After the first day she contacted me, I deleted the request only for her to send another picture the next day. He must have really put it on her. This cheating scandal ended up becoming a large issue with several others at Ethan's job. After the first day of him getting caught cheating, the next few days we did not speak. No one said a word. There was no humbling moment, no sorry, no I was wrong. Complete silence.

About a week later, we were in his vehicle the same vehicle he was posing in the pictures with, I asked him something about the situation, and he blew up again! I guess it was just best for me to leave the subject alone. He said he never slept with her, but I know better. I had even found the pictures in his email inbox and printed them. I do not even know where they are now, but I had them.

I later learned that the girl ended up not working at his job no longer and that she tried to contact him to apologize. I showed them to my two closest friends at the time Jessica and Kristy. Therefore, they can be witnesses if needed. A few of my friends did not care for Ethan. Although they were supportive, they did not care for him neither did my mother. My mother loved him because I loved him, and she loves me. When the pillow talk Ethan and I shared began showing in his actions towards my family. I was caught between a rock and a hard place.

I was hearing grief from my mom and sister about how disrespectful he was, and he did not make them feel welcome in our marital home. This went on for years even though we spent two Christmases together blending and getting to know each other prior to us getting married. After we got married, I was happy! That was very short lived. Ethan and I continued to have our life outside of each other and then we would do some couple of outings but not much.

During the marriage, I was still traveling and visiting friends and we were just two people who were married but we never quiet joined as one. I changed my last name, and it did not faze him, one bit. I wanted a bank account together he did not, I wanted us to watch our wedding DVD and look at our photo album often, he did not. I also wanted us to renew our vows after five or 10 years, he would not hear of it. When it came to visiting my family in California, if I wanted him to go therefore, I had to pay for his ticket. If I wanted us to go on a trip I had to plan and pay for it. That was exhausting and it was like pulling teeth with someone who is supposed to be your better half.

Another thing that I do not miss is being talked about physically. I always took pride in how I looked, but my husband did not appreciate it and never complimented me on anything. I can probably count on two hands how many times I have actually heard that from him. I absolutely love how I can just get up, put clothes on, and not have to worry about how I look and if he would look at me crazy. I have always been a make-up girl, so who wants to heat that they look like they are going to the prom every day.

He was trying to tear me down and it worked a little bit. I mentally fought daily to dispel his lack of empathy or affection be my issue. I remember one time the insurance agent was at our house, and we signed up for a policy. We got on the subject of weight and the man said you look good for having two children and he gave a look to the man as if he were saying no she does not. The man said come on man. I was SO embarrassed that my husband would say that to another man.

A few years ago, I was cleaning up my laptop to give to my niece and found a journal entry dated in 2011 where I stated that I was unhappy. This was 2 years after we got married. There I was in shock once again. Which brings me to my own cheating scandal. I began talking on the phone and chatting with other men during the marriage. I also ended up sleeping with a few of them. I did not want to, but I am craving to feel desired and needed. I was searching for something that I did not have in my marriage. That is not an excuse, because I was fully aware of what I did, it is just a result of a lifeless loveless marriage.

I do not look for a man to make me happy but he damn sure cannot be the reason for my unhappiness. A man should complement you do not complete you. A husband should protect you and allow you to feel safe and secure within the relationship of marriage. A man nor a husband should not tear you down by making you feel worthless by asking you if you are going to prom because you put on make-up. He should not say after having two children less than six months after your second child in 2 ½ years that you still look 4 months pregnant. After I gave birth to our daughter, I was feeling just ok. It was an adjustment by this being my first child. There were many meltdowns internally.

I say internally because I shut that part of my brain and total being down. I suffered in silence because when I did express how I felt because my feelings were not acknowledged and was shunned by my husband. I was too sensitive, crazy, or bipolar. He labeled me every mental illness there was known to man. Right after I had gotten a routine down pat with Reagan and with him working nights. In April of 2015, I found out that I was having another baby in December of 2015 and that is when depression sat in.

Depression plagued me throughout my pregnancy. As much as I like to celebrate and have events. I had no desire to have a baby shower. One of my close friends finally convinced me to have a "Ladies Lunch" in which is what I called it. I let her plan the entire thing because I had no interest in being my usual controlling self. This depression caused some friendship to take a drastic turn for the worse. However, I had no energy to entertain that issue at the time. I was emotionally drowning. I do not expect anyone to relate unless you chose to.

It is like a sinkhole that you can see yourself in, but hard as hell to climb out. I am usually the firefighter who helps others climb out of their depression/emotional state. There was no one that could help to climb out because I was unaware of how deep the debt sinkhole was. No one putting food or water in the hole. The person in the hole is still in there giving all she can until she has no more energy left to give.

My depression lasted well after my son was born. At this point, it is beginning to affect how my husband treats and talks to me even more so. He started by saying things such as the kids like me more than you and the kids are more attached to me than they are to you, and I asked Reagan who she has more fun with and she told me meaning him. I told him I do not give a flying fuck about being the fun parent. I am the parent who reads to them, buys educational toys, and locates the best doctors and schools for my children. His sole purpose is to control the children and buy them toys. In my opinion material things that will not matter in years to come.

Spring 2016, after my son was born. Ethan came to me stating that he had found my dream vehicle. My dream vehicle was a maroon Lexus RX 350 with peanut butter interior. I absolutely loved that car. However, there was a catch as always with him. He proposed that I give his parents my current vehicle and to get my car in which I did just that for my family.

The summer of 2016 is when he came home with a luxury vehicle, and I was livid. I had called him that evening to check in and he said nothing about being at a dealership. I did not speak to him for days. I told myself he has no respect for me. I eventually got over it, as he knew I would. We were soon leaving for vacation, so I sucked it up. We finally got some alone time as his parents went with us on vacation. We sat down and I asked him about the vehicle and how much was the payment. He preceded to tell me that it was none of my business and that I was not paying for it. Now, at this time, his parents are driving my other car and he was supposed to be paying the note. Not paying the note on a new car for himself.

I started going through the office making copies of tax returns, W2's credit cards. Every night I found some new information. I found all of the credit cards he applied for in my name. I was flabbergasted. I also found out that the Harley Davidson motorcycle was paid for and that I had gotten for him was sold. He had me do a title pawn and said he needed money for the mortgage but never paid on it and the title pawnshop sold it. I was such a nice cruiser that he took pride in or so I thought. I asked him how the payment was going, and he said it is going well. I had not heard him mention anything about it. About a week later, I called, and they said that they sold it a few months back. When I questioned him about it, he said I knew you would find out anyway. That hurt.

I filed for divorce in August of 2017. Ethan was served divorce papers about a week prior to me moving September 2017. My last week in the home was horrific. I refused to talk to him because all he wanted to do was argue and be pissed off. I began packing and plotting to leave.

Scare Tactics

When dealing with a narcissist they try any and every type of scare tactic. Approximately 2 weeks after I moved out, we had a hurricane Irma came through Atlanta, Georgia on September 10, 2017. My power went out for about 3-4 days. I was asked and obliged to stay with my soon to be ex-husband. Not only was I dealing with the adjustment of moving out only to move back into the marital home even though it was a temporary situation it was the most comforting space that I could be in given the circumstances.

Here I am at the martial home sleeping on the couch that I had been sleeping on for months so that was not a big deal. However, the next day was our eighth-year wedding anniversary. My soon to be ex-brings home 2 greeting cards stating how much he loved me. Everyone that knows me knows that I absolutely love greeting cards. I love to give them and receive them. He was trying to speak to me in that manner. Ethan wanted me to rescind divorce. I said no. A few days later, he asked me to do the divorce uncontested. I said no. Then, he threatened to tell people we know about my medical history and personal occurrences between us. I said that I did not care. He was livid.

I was no longer his supply nor was he able to control me in the way he had in the decade prior. I was slowly starting to see the destruction that he started to impose on me. He did what he could to tear me down physically by stating I should not wear and how my stomach looked after carrying our two children. He also would question me if I was going to prom in regard to why I would put on make-up in which I loved wearing. Many of the horrific instances would randomly pop up in my head as I go through my healing phases.

September 2017, a year after I moved out of the marital home, I felt joy and an overwhelming amount of unspeakable peace. The common saying that state a peace of mind is priceless is a complete understatement. No longer was I the supply of a leach. As I sit here today after almost 5 years of being "narc free" I feel as a weight has been lifted off me. In

Now 4 years post-divorce I started to dissect the lessons I learned while in the marriage and after the marriage. When I left in September 2017, I was emotionally and financially bankrupt. I did not have anything to give anyone. I began to drink heavily. I would sleep when the kids were with their father and after about a good 6-12 months of this. I was through. I was as if I have to make myself eat, get out of the house and do something different with my off time.

If it were not for the divorce, I probably would not be in the creative space that I am currently experiencing. September of 2018, I said, I am going get my passion back. I began calling around to different spa's looking for Esthetician openings. I finally landed on Oasis Massage they called me right after I left a voicemail message. I worked there from September 2018 to June 2018. Knowing that that was a stepping-stone, I began buying my spa equipment with the money I was making on the side. That is how I began my company Face-up Skincare Salon, LLC.

The most positive things that I can say about my "Assignment" (aka marriage) is that I learned that I must follow my passion, by any means necessary. Regardless of how I feel emotionally or physically, I still have to do it scared. It did not matter what the start looks like, the goal was to just start. For me, "the start" meant getting back to myself after the kids, starting to enjoy myself and loving myself again, asking myself what I wanted, whether it was starting my own business, making a much-needed counseling appointment, writing a book, creating a book club, and exercising. I cannot even begin to express how many times I have falsely started my spa business.

Whether starting was getting back to myself after kids, starting to enjoy and love me, asking myself "what do you want?," start the business, make the counseling appointment, write the book, start the club, exercise. I cannot even begin to express how many different times I have wanted to start my spa business.

My assignment of my first marriage was to learn that neither one of us were ready for marriage. In my opinion, I got married because he asked, and I wanted a life of stability. I believe he asked me simply because that was one of my conditions to getting back together along with a baby. He did exactly what I wanted him to do nothing more and nothing less. In conclusion, I learned that you cannot tell a person one thing and expect another without proper communication. I learned what crutches I used to cope, to lean on therapy and to do the work, I learned that when you have hit rock bottom emotionally, the only place left is to grow up and out from under all of the dirt. I believe I received an A+ on the assignment of life after divorce.

My Chain Breaking Words for You: Do it scared!

APA Reference

Tracy, N. (2012). Emotional Abuse: Definitions, Signs, Symptoms, Examples, HealthyPlace. Retrieved on 2019, November 26 from https://www.healthyplace.com/abuse/emotional-psychological-abuse/emotional-abuse-definitions-signs-symptoms-examples

About TaMara Sewell-Craig

TaMara Craig is the owner & operator of Face-Up Skin Care Salon,

LLC. She has a passion for skin care and educating people about their skin, so much so that she became a Licensed Esthetician in 2006 and an Esthetician Instructor in 2021. In 2019, TaMara founded and created *Face-Up Skin Care Salon* where she specializes in healthy skin care, acne, dermaplaning, waxing and much more.

Currently, she teaches part-time at Lovett Beauty School and is a community volunteer as needed. TaMara is a graduate of Shorter University with a master's degree in Organizational Leadership and is a United States Army Veteran. Last but certainly not least, TaMara the proud wife of Mr. Victor Craig, mother of 2, and an entrepreneur who hails from Ontario, California.

15

LOOK THE OTHER WAY

Heather Cain Wisenbaker

U.S. Air Force Veteran

I am standing in the middle of the room screaming...." CAN YOU HEAR ME?" Why does everyone look the other way? "You don't see him touching my hair, rubbing my shoulder! YOU don't hear him speak utter sickness to me? HELLO, DO YOU SEE ME?"

You all laugh as he leaves the room, so of course you saw and heard, and as each laugh strums my ears it victimizes me again and again! "DO YOU SEE ME? Why is this funny?" Others say, "Oh just get used to it, he didn't cross the line. If you report this, you will ruin your career, they won't believe you." Eighteen months of burying the trauma he causes every time he sees me, every time he shows his face at the dorms. My life becomes a doormat for him to wipe his feet on because he can; he's the boss.

My biggest concern each day at work is to stay clear of him. I'm lost. I have no one to help me be brave against him. His wife watched one evening at a squadron event as he started coming on to me. Can you imagine the horror and embarrassment for her and for me? What an Asshole!

Eighteen months later, I came forward with a detailed statement of everything he did to me. I was forced to report to my commander, as I walked into his office there stood a line of leaders, all male, just standing there listening to me, to intimidate me. Did they think I would get scared and run away? As my CO began to yell at me, "Who do you think you are?" I began to lose control and tears of anger and frustration ran down my checks. With all the strength of God, I looked him in the eye as calmly as I could, said, "Is this how you would treat your daughter if she reported this to you?" His silence and my leadership's silence could cut glass, and yet again, THEY LOOKED AWAY.

I was 24. What did I know? So, I buried this anger. The hate I carried for those leaders and that time of my life began changing me. Why didn't anyone help me and stand up for me? With age and wisdom, I got louder, began to lose the fear of not being believed, being isolated.

Still today, 24 years later, it still can stir up so much internally. Someone says something or a memory comes along that makes me want to run to that young woman and hug her and tell her she should have never had to deal with that abuse.

Daily I tell myself, never LOOK AWAY, never BE QUIET, stand up and be heard. You are worthy, and in time the chains of trauma will crack.

My Chain Breaking Words for You:

In order to rise, you must get out of your way! Once you face your fear, you'll look back and laugh at how long it took you to just JUMP!

About Heather Cain Wisenbaker

Heather Cain Wisenbaker is an entrepreneur, wife & mother. Retired from the United States Air Force, Security Forces. She served in Operation Enduring Freedom, Operation Iraqi Freedom, and Operation Northern/Southern Watch during her service. She's a wife and mother & resides outside of San Antonio. She works from home while homeschooling her autistic 9-year-old. Heather is a Florida native and loves the beach. She is the self-published children's author of *The Sweet Tooth Goblin*, story of the Tooth Fairy & her mischievous Tooth Goblins. Her passion is to mentor and coach women, empowering them to find their inner beauty and strength.

16

THE STRUGGLE HAS THE MOST BEAUTIFUL OUTCOMES

G.I. Shane

U.S. Army Veteran

Land of the free, huh? My whole life, that's what I've been told. Yet, nothing worth it has ever been free for me. Pain and depression, look at her expression. Just another abandoned adolescent. With a stolen innocence that paid for her family's lifestyle. She wasn't Brenda with a baby, nor was fancy her name, instead, it was G.I. Shane.

I didn't always know I was going to be a Soldier, but I *always* knew I was going to make something of my life. I wanted better, I became a mother at 15, my childhood was traumatic at times, and those traumas carried over into my adult life.

I was raised not to talk about the "ugly" things in life because when you do, then you're labeled as being negative or if you're a faith-based individual, you're looked at like you're not trusting in God.

No, my friend, you talk about the ugly, so history doesn't repeat itself.

I was never addicted to alcohol or drugs, but I had an addiction. I thought I had to be "perfect." For over 20 years of my life, I perfected "never wearing my worries." My Abuelita would always tell me that when I was sad. She'd say, "Never wear your worries, Mijita, it'll age you before your time." So, I learned how to smile. I look at pictures from my past and think to myself "you're smiling but the night before you barely slept, or you just had your heart shattered. Your photos always told a different story, the one you didn't want others to know." In about 60% of my pictures, something tragic had happened but you'd never know it unless you truly knew me. I had no clue the price I'd pay for "never wearing your worries." It was a lot of sacrifice and restraint.

I was being raised by "Sunday only" Christians. You know, the kind of people who Monday through Saturday were hell on wheels, drinking, partying, getting high, etc.… My confusion about who God really was started at a very early age. I really questioned God's love for me.

One earth-guide God blessed me with was my mother's mother. My Abuelita taught me to listen to my woman's' and mothers' intuition, to rely on my inner spirit and let it be my inspiration for myself, family and all I love. My life, up until about 2 years ago seriously felt like a real *Lifetime* series, and the chaos was never ending. I literally stopped asking God what was next at one point in my life, I personally felt like God was taking my prayers as challenges.

Elders around me were always encouraging me to pray and trust God's plan for me. I began to not want people around me. If one more person told me to have faith and pray, I was gonna scream. Then one day it hit me; I was praying but I was not putting anything into works.

Around the same time, I remember watching the Vanessa Guillen story. Looking at her and myself in our dress blues made me realize, I was her. Unlike Vanessa and countless others, I survived. It was important for my story to get out, but I only wanted to run away from life. A friend told me I was a victim and it pissed me off! He then told me once I accepted that I'd become a victor. That became the "it" for me, no more excuses it was time to let my voice be heard. I had to remember my training and how I was taught to stand my ground. To do that I had to dig deep and confront the things that were holding me back. I had to admit and acknowledge the hurts and pains caused by myself and others.

As a child I was called womanish and a hoe by my mother so much so that at one point in my life as a young woman, I felt offering my body to men was the only way I was going to receive or give love. I was molested as a young girl and looking back I feel like the adults in my life turned blind eyes to afford their lifestyle.

At a very early age I lost me because of the hateful, negative and expressed opinions of those around me who deposited negativity in my mind by telling me I wasn't worth anything. People took my kindness as a weakness. Failing to see my kindness wasn't because I was weak, rather my kindness was because I saw something weak in them in the first place. I struggled and fought for a long time within. I lost myself with negative words and thought I was ugly. Over the years, people have always complimented me on looks. I honestly can't remember a time where someone hadn't made a comment about my looks. When I looked in a mirror the reflection I saw was that of devastation.

Insecurities convinced me that I was worthless, ugly, and that no one would ever love me for me or through intimacy. As a mature woman of God, I now know that it was because of what my family and others had spoken negatively over and into my life that had me feeling that way. I grew up with people hurting all the time and as most people know - hurt people hurt people. Experiencing what I did as a child and young woman made me more compassionate. I learned very quickly to be cautious of what I spoke over and into my children's lives. Even if I couldn't control others around them, I could control myself. I didn't always succeed. I also broke bloodline and generational curses and chains.

Chains broke for me when I went into the Army. My Abuelita passed away when I was 23 and my foundation was rocked to the core. I knew I had to do something to show my sons a better way of life. The direction I was going in at that time made me feel like I was just going to be a drug dealer's girlfriend my whole life. I thought people would be supportive, but it was the exact opposite. My own mother told me I was just trying to go into the Army so I didn't have to take care of my children. I even remember I was receiving food stamps and childcare and when I went to talk to my case worker and give her my ship out date and ask her to close my case, she said "I'll keep it here for when you come back."

Right before I went into the military, I prayed one night, and I asked God what to do. I couldn't figure out any other way at the moment to get myself in a better financial position so that my sons could have better. I got this overwhelming urge to write a letter as I was praying, I began to type on my computer, and I was crying so hard I don't know how I typed but when I was done the letter was from God to me. And this is what it said:

Shanell,

For unto you on this day I have released a newfound peace in your life. My dearest daughter all of your worries you will cast aside, on my command. Peace is unto you, your family and all of those you hold dear to your heart. On my command your enemies have fled, for I have shed my blood onto you.

Through you a new beauty will empower you. A beauty that is not physical but spiritual.

A new wisdom has been released to you. No longer will you be cautious with your decisions.

I am your strength, your mother, your father, your lover, your husband saith the Lord.

This storm shall pass and with the calm of the storm I will set forth gold at your feet. In which you will find the independence and encouragement you so strongly seek. Peace be unto your children. I am their father; I will guide your boys into men. Through you they will serve me. I have called them by name before they were born, do not be afraid.

Your journey will be peaceful. You will shine like you have never shown do not fear your separation will not be long. I have already sent you a Man, to guide you, nurture, and love… Do not stray from the path I have set in place. Be obedient to me my child. I have loved you and will always love you like no other. I know all of your dreams they are but small steps away. Stand proud my daughter, dry your tears. You are in my arms and in my heart.

-GOD

After that letter, I ran. I went into the Army as a cook. When arriving in basic, the Army cut the LL's off my name and I had no middle name so on paper I looked like a man. I wasn't G.I. Jane; I was G.I. Shane. My sons were always what I fought so hard for. Even if it didn't make sense to anyone around me, I knew I had to show them how a woman could be strong and still be feminine. Here I was a 24-year-old woman who left 3 children at home against everyone's protests. For the first time in my life, I found myself completely alone. Just me and hundreds of other individuals all thrown together to train.

Basic was challenging mentally more so than physically. It helped me heal from many childhood traumas. I finally learned to love myself, with every challenge that came my way and I conquered. My walk with God got even stronger.

One challenge was during weapons qualifications. All week long I was shooting *great*. The ultimate goal was to get 40 out of 40 shots. However, you only needed 23 to qualify. Come qualification day, I was pumped and ready to go! I went out onto the range, got to my lane, set myself up, and I shot a 22. No worries I could go again, but my hopes of being more than a marksman were gone for the moment. I went out to qualify a second time and I shot a 22, I went out a third time and I shot a 22. I was pissed, so pissed tears were falling. I remember one of the drill sergeants told me it was ok, that the day wasn't over. The Chaplain came around and asked if there were any Soldiers who hadn't qualified if we might be interested in saying a quick prayer. All of a sudden about 60-70 Soldiers dropped to one knee, it was so serene. The Chaplain prayed for all of us, and I was extremely pumped. So, I went on the range for a fourth time, and I shot an 18, I was completely baffled and beyond frustrated. This is NOT the result I expected especially after praying. I felt like "God are you listening or are you playing with me?" I remember a Colonel coming by and giving us a "pep" talk. I remember sitting off to the side at the basin of a tree. I put my head on my knees and started praying. I asked God to give me my grandmother's strength. For we used to call her Granny MacGyver – she could fix ANYTHING, from her car to a lamp chord fixture, plumbing, cook, crochet the most beautiful dollies and sew the most beautiful clothes. I just knew if she was with me in some way, I'd be ok.

So out to the range I went, for the last time of the day, and so much was riding on me passing. If I didn't pass with my company, I'd be recycled with another company when they went to the range. No one who has been to the range wants that to happen. As I got into the fox hole to prepare myself, I looked down range and saw the top of the trees swaying back and forth gently. It was a Heat Category 5 that day as well, which means it was hot as hell! There was no wind or anything. As I was looking at the top of the trees, the trees started swaying back and forth gently. I could literally feel God's presence at that moment. After fixing my foxhole, I looked at my weapon on the butt of my weapon was a monarch butterfly. I KNEW at that moment my grandmother was with me, for monarchs were one of her favorites. Not only did I qualify that round, but I was the top shooter. And even though I didn't get a sharpshooter badge, I was proud of myself. I grew spiritually and emotionally once again. I knew God was with me and so was my grandmother's spirit.

At the end of basic I won an award in basic for ministering. It wasn't necessarily religious ministering; I was just able to communicate effectively with the Drill Sergeants and could assist Soldiers quickly. So, the Base Chaplain asked me if I'd be interested in becoming a Chaplain Assistant. Naïve me thought I was just going to be a secretary for the Chaplain. I wish I had just been a secretary (Lol). I had to be knowledgeable in all the major religions the military recognized and provide religious support, counseling, and service set ups for Soldiers and their families. On top of that I was the Chaplain's bodyguard. I had to protect this man or woman at all costs no matter religion. Chaplain Assistant School made basic look like a cake walk. I had to educate myself on all these different religions, and I was not raised that way.

I came from Bible Belt, middle USA, and Christianity was it. Now there were Baptist, Pentecostals, Southern Baptists and Nondomination churches I grew up in. Trying to read about Catholics, Buddhists, Muslims and Judaism was like listening to Charlie Brown's teacher. I couldn't grasp a thing and if I didn't, I was gonna fail and have to go to a different MOS. I remember calling my aunt, who I knew to be one of the most Bible-fearing individuals I knew. I remember her telling me that I needed to look at it like being a Soldier. My aunt was the furthest thing from a Soldier, I didn't know where she was going with this. I knew not say anything but to just listen. I'm glad I did. She said

"Shanell, what do Soldiers do before battle? You study the terrain, people, religion and customs, not to convert, but to educate yourself for battle." That was it for me again. I soaked up everything like a sponge and was extremely successful.

God revealed himself to me shortly after that. I had a battle buddy I would invite to pray with myself and a few other Chaplain Assistants. Every night she had an excuse to not come and join us. One night after coming back from praying I found a note on my bed. My battle wrote "Smitty, I really respect you and value our friendship. So, I don't know how you're gonna take this but the reason I never join you or the girls to pray is I am wiccan." Reading that letter made me feel no different about her. In fact, I realized how much courage she had to come to me and tell that. It was still the don't ask policy era, so I was proud of her, and I told her so about 2 years into my service, I received a letter from my battle buddy who had gotten out of the Service. She told that all my prayers must have worked because she had converted over to Christianity and thanked me for never judging her. I still think of her and pray for her to this day.

Shortly after Chaplain Assistant school I went back to my state. I was assigned to an Aviation Battalion. Ironically enough our unit crest said, "We defend from above." Once again, I thought God was joking with me. Soon after arriving to my unit, we started preparing for deployment. During our final SRP (Soldier Readiness Program), it was discovered that my medical records were missing. The doctor saw a scar on my back and asked me about it and I told him I'd had back surgery prior to entering into the military. I had to get a medical congressional to join the military. The doctor changed my PHULES code, making me nondeployable.

I was so angry. I had been training and preparing with my unit and now my battles would be without me. While speaking to a sergeant in S-1, a specialist approached me and asked me if I'd be interested in a team he was putting together. I would go to school to become a Tabbed Military Funerals Honor Guard Team Soldier for the State of Kansas. I'd get put on orders and it would consist of a lot of drill and ceremony. So, I said yes, and off to Honor Guard School I went.

I remember walking into class feeling so overwhelmed, here were all these men, combat veterans, infantry men, engineers and here I was this 5'2" probably looking like a miss priss, but I was the most ghetto etiquette country gal they EVER met!!!I definitely felt intimidated, but I had a skill they needed. The night before graduation we were getting our uniforms ready and a few of the guys needed their pants hemmed. I told them I could hem them. I just couldn't get my uniform ready and theirs at the same time. So, we started a small line and gott'er done! We all passed inspection and graduated the next day. Thank God for Abuelita's sewing skills.

Becoming the first female to serve on the Kansas Military Funerals Honor Guard Team was phenomenal. Most people when I tell them what I did always respond with "I'm sorry," or "that must've been so hard." It wasn't at all. What I learned is that everybody dies, but not everybody lives. I had the upmost pleasure and honor to listen to countless little ordinary looking old men and women's, life stories, accomplishments, unimaginable heroism and bravery. I got to bring my sons along their summer breaks. They got to watch my team and I perform. I got to serve alongside some of the most honorable and respectable men I have ever had the pleasure of meeting in my life. Without each of them in their own ways, I definitely wouldn't be the woman I have been blessed to become. They taught me about my strength and dignity. When my crown tilted each of one in one way or another reminded me to adjust it and keep pushing forward. Even battles who I never served on the Honor Guard Team with taught me about my strengths and always encouraged me when I was wavering. I had a village. Until one day my village was rocked.

I got hurt in an accident and trying to be the "Super Soldier" I thought I had to be I pushed myself. It was one of the hardest things ever in my life. Again, God was preparing me. Trying to push myself and get back to being an Honor Guard Soldier, I didn't take my meds properly.

I couldn't be on some of them and be on duty. During a field exercise I passed out from my blood pressure rising so high from being in pain. I had to go to the ER. A medic I knew was going to take me, but the unit doctor had another medic from another company take me instead. I was taken to the ER and then the medic took me back to our sleeping quarters. I remember he took me to get my meds filled and took me to my room. At my room things got very ugly very quickly.

This medic assaulted me, and I could not fight back. I tried and I fought as hard as I could but being incapacitated with medications left me weak. At some point I passed out, and when I woke up in the morning, he was lying in my bed next to me. I was covered in bruises and confused, scared and ashamed suddenly. Trying to piece everything together and grasp what had just happened to me. I remember the medic got up and acted like everything was normal. As if we were in a relationship and were buddies. I was able to go to the bathroom and I locked myself in the bathroom. He eventually left.

My battle buddy who was supposed to be staying in my room, came in. She saw him leave our room, I remember her knocking on the bathroom door and asking me if I was okay. If I needed to talk to her, she was there for me. I cleaned myself up and did what I always did when something tragic happened, I put a smile on my face. I told her I was fine. I remember her grabbing my hand and looking me in my eyes and she said "Shanell, I am here. If you want to talk, I will help you. I went through the same thing." Me being me, I tried to play it off.

Everything in me was screaming to open my mouth and say something. Yet something in me had broken and triggered extreme sadness, shame, and embarrassment. I went numb and silent. All the things my training taught me not to do for some reason, I did. I lost all sense of what I was supposed to do for myself. I literally withdrew from everyone. I was lost and did not want to acknowledge what had happened. I felt like a failure. I felt abandoned by God. How could he allow me to get hurt? How could I not fight back?

I went down a serious rabbit whole. It didn't help that I started losing my loved ones, my "foundation" at the same time I was losing Soldiers to suicide. I witnessed some of their suicides. My battle who found me committed suicide. I didn't even know it because I was so lost in my own life. I lost track of time and I stopped reaching out. Drugs and alcohol never were a problem because if that had been it would have been *way* worse. Choices are truly what saved me in life, learning to listen, to take each tragedy and find the lessons and blessings. Then focus on the blessing. I had to relearn so many things. I had to stop beating myself up about everything that went wrong in my life and learn to focus on everything that went right.

Every time I thought God wasn't there, he really was it just wasn't in the manner I thought it should be. Once I was a young girl with a baby at 15, then I was the first child out of my parents to get a high school diploma. My parents had my older brother at a very young age and dropped out of high school. I broke that generational curse of illiteracy. Each one of my sons through MANY prayers, tears and sacrifices graduated high school with no children. Breaking the chain of teen pregnancy. I have a son who has mental health issues. With the training and knowledge, I received as a Chaplain Assistant, I have been able to stand in the gap and effectively communicate many times to assist him in getting care. To educate and advocate individuals with mental health issues. I thank God he knew what I needed even when I doubted him.

In my journey of finding me after the military, after being attacked. I found my voice again. I am most thankful to have learned so far that the struggle has the most beautiful outcomes even if they don't make sense at times. I hope as you have read this, you find yourself and you find your own strength. I hope anyone who reads this will know that they are not alone.

You heal by releasing not suppressing. I pray you become unchained whether you are a Veteran or not, and you to learn to break the cycles of trauma one link at a time.

My Chain Breaking Words for You:

Psalm 107: 14 "He brought them out of darkness, the utter darkness, and broke away their chains."

About G.I. Shane

G.I. Shane was raised and born in Kansas. She graduated high school in 1996. She went to college, then after the birth of her 3rd son and losing her grandmother, G.I. Shane joined the Army. G.I. Shane briefly served active duty Army, then went to the Kansas Army National Guard where she made history and became the 1st Tabbed Female to Serve on the 1st Kansas Military Funerals Honor Guard Team for the State of Kansas.

17

THE DATE:
A LESSON NOT LOST

Wilfreda Waller

U.S. Army Veteran

Warning: chapter comes with tears…..

Man…I can't believe I'm telling this story! For decades I've held onto this secret inside the torn, and desolate crevasses of my mind and heart. I've talked to Yahweh in counsel, of the way I should tell what happened to me when I served in the United States Army over twenty years ago. Here goes…….

One Morning it was a beautiful, sunny morning, fresh out of high school I'd made the decision to join the military: it was August of 1979. It was about 10:00 a.m. one morning when I got enough courage to go see the recruiter. There I was, this polished city girl from Detroit, full of life and expectancy. It was at that moment when I said "I do" to the Military Oath, which sealed my condemned fate for a long time. As I take a glance back to the time, let me just say it would serve each incoming soldier a great deal of justice on the front end of recruitment to have some sort of recruitment counseling, so one can understand the full scope of what will happen; what to expect. If someone had directed path on the recruitment process, then I would have been a savvier selectee than the selected. I started off my military career in National Guard then later volunteered to go full active duty but was met with major resistance when I got to my duty station. The Military Admin had this thing going, that anybody that came into active duty from National Guard, they assume was forced to join active duty as a punishment. There I was, ignorant and unprotected from a system of which I was about to get a horrific taste.

I remember telling the recruiter that I wanted to pursue something in a secretarial "typing job." I must have sealed the recruiter's fate in meeting his quota, because he did not hesitate to offer this position to me which was Tele-Type-Communications Operator (72ECO). I remember my feelings at that moment in time. I felt accomplished, patriotic, and proud to serve my country. I thought I was going to have a career. I thought I would be happy with my job choice. I thought I was set for life! The recruiter mentioned that this MOS could be tactical or stationary, but that he decided to enlist me in the tactical side of the

MOS. This MOS was designed to set up and maintain tactical communication for an Infantry Battalion Division playing war games. Little did I know, the day I swore and reinstated myself into volunteer active-duty service would be the horizon of the darkest days of my life for a long time. See, I did not understand the wording "tactical." This meant that you were going to train, eat, sleep for the whole infantry division and be around a particular class of men. Living alongside these infantry men! The recruiter also failed to disclose that in a tactical unit, a female was to perform 95% of her job in the field. That meant, your whole existence was maintained in the field supporting infantry battalions exercising war games. I had to have my periods in the field and wash my bloody ass in a combat helmet for a bath. That meant I had to spend 28 days out of 30 in a disgusting, filthy, wooded or desert area. I'm just being honest, and trust me when I say, this is *not* what I believed I signed up for. I later found out that these infantry men, during the 1960-1970's, were given a choice as to under what conditions they could join. It was very common for men to be offered to sign up for the military to avoid jail time, and the powers that be are considering reinstating this practice.. This is where my story begins because I had to interact with these 'criminal-minded" individuals.

I remember feeling desperately lonely. I was away from family, and I had no friends or allies.

I remember one day, back at the barracks, I was sitting on bleachers on an Army parade field and these two infantrymen were walking by. One decided to strike up a conversation with me. I remember the one guy that was talking to me was extremely cute and I felt like a schoolgirl because he chose to talk with me. I remember as I was getting dressed, I thought to myself, "could this man be my future husband?" I was just that lonely. Holding onto any scraps of hope in the newfound cruel world known as the military. As I recall, we went to the on-post club and had a drink, and good chemistry, but this is where it gets obtuse. I really can't recall going to his room, but that's where I ended up. I believe the soldier put a mickey in my drink. All I can say is at this point, after doing the sex deed, I recall him saying he was going to the rest room. I remember closing my eyes for a little bit before I felt him (I thought it was him, my date) crawling into bed with me. I turned towards him to let him know I wanted to go and at that precise moment, I knew I had looked into the eyes of the devil. It was a completely different person! He was black as midnight and reminded me of a monster; something I would detest! He was attempting to try and have intercourse with me, but I refused and that's when he got on top of me, and I started to scream. I was screaming and fighting him off me. I managed to leap up out of the bed, still screaming and frantic. I was looking for my clothes. I was naked, but these men had hidden my clothes. I remember my heart dropped at that discovery, that my clothes were missing. I then ran to the door, opened it and was still screaming and butt ass naked I cried out for help, but no one came to my rescue. He pulled me back in the room still trying to rape me. That's when I grabbed a white t-shirt, and I began to climb out a window. I was on the second floor of the building, and at least 30 feet up. I recall climbing out and my thought process was to shimmy down a waterspout pipe alongside the building to safety. Instead, the pipe was not able to hold my weight at that point, making me free falling some 30-25 feet. I remember my screams on the way down in the free fall. I hit the ground with an impact that left me with instant injuries. I'm remembering my tailbone, right foot with immediate and excruciating pain, so much so that I could not stand. The pain was too unbearable. I couldn't walk, so I had to crawl to my barracks, at least two buildings over 700 yards away. I was crawling as best I could, crying still, and in total disbelief. I was naked under the t-shirt and scared the two men were after me. I was in escape mode. I remember finally getting to my barracks and did not want the night watchman of my barracks to see me, so I attempted to get into my room through a window. The window was too high, and I was too injured, and after a few failed attempts, the guy that I originally had the date with appeared with my clothes and asked me what happened. I couldn't even look at him. He just dropped clothes and ran off into the night.

With extreme difficulty I was able to put my clothes on and hobbled into my barracks to the best of my ability. I was asked over and over what happened, but I could not say it. I could not even begin to describe the horrific trauma and turbulent scene I had just gone through. My battalion company had to call an ambulance for me because I could not walk. When the smoke cleared that night in the hospital, I had a busted ankle, and busted tailbone, and lower back injuries, and I needed stitches in my middle finger because my finger got caught on a nail on the way down during my free fall and ripped it open. The flashbacks are unreal, I'm scared to sleep because of my "military dreams" I call them. Because of all the immense trauma, I had to endure my entire military time. I even married an infantry man, which is a book unto itself. He was infantry and I would later discover, I married Lucifer.

Because of the isolation a woman feels while in an unhealthy environment in the military, again, scared and alone, I moved subdued, understated and restrained throughout the rest of time serving in the military. Even though this book project is bringing back the traumatic memories, effects, and affairs.

This is a very cathartic project for me. God placed this book project on my heart a long time ago, and I give thanks for this opportunity. I get it, the "broken chains" and what the women of the book project need to do moving forward, but can I be honest? I have suffered so much trauma at the hands of the Army and being married to military man that even though I do feel a sense of release of this traumatic event, to a certain degree, my trauma is so deeply imbedded that I feel it is going to take all my life to work on my life and finally escape the chains of trauma that bind me.

I'm a work in progress. I can say this, nowadays, I can say I've joined a new Army; it's called GOD'S ARMY!

I honestly believe that my story will help other women who join the military make much better decisions about their career choices.

Knowing that I'm doing God's calling on my life as I advocate to raise awareness.

The Heavenly Father has placed some wonderful women in my life through this anthology. They are helping me come out of the darkness of trauma and step into the light of healing. So, I urge each and every one, that has been a victim of MST(military sexual trauma) please contact, your local /female support group and start telling. This support group connection will in turn make other connections to get you all the assistance you will need. In closing, look; at the statistics!

What does trauma look like for you? I ask the women reading this book, because in all my 61 years of living I have uncovered a disastrous truth. Women, by far experience trauma the stats will shock you. According to the RAINN report (Rape, Abuse & Incest National Network), 9 out of every 10 victims of rape are female. That's 90% female: 17.7 million American Women as of 1998. The female population around the globe still endures some type of sexual trauma, young and old.

But my dear women, I would implore you to trust and know that the same 90% of women, who had to suffer, you can also know that we as a collective unique group share something else, that's an almost magical resilience to persevere through it all. Patiently waiting for your triumph as a victim no more. This takes time and it will happen for you, just like triumph from victim to victorious, finally breaking the chain link of trauma happened for me. Break the link of the silence, embarrassment, mental anguish, physical pain, secrecy, struggle, disappointment, disrespect, anger, hate…yes, your resilience, my sister. I urge each of you to break each link that is incumbent on each woman's individual strengths. I can urge each of you to break each link slowly and methodically. You want through this change leaving no piece unturned.

My Chain Breaking Words for You:

Individually, we must all fight collectively. Get angry and unapologetically reject the bullshit life will offer you.

About Wilfreda Waller

Meet Wilfreda Waller: my 4 children and 5 beautiful grandchildren are my legacy. They are my life. Determined to make a difference, I'm devoted to raising awareness with women soldiers of all branches of the military. As sisters in arms and sisters in Christ, enlightening others using my past military life experiences is my life's calling. I will forge ahead for my sisters, prayerfully, out of the darkness of MST into a continued space of awareness and enlightenment, in turn, leading you to strength, victory and peace.

Possessing deep compassion to advocate for my fellow sister veterans/soldiers, my writing focuses on the awareness that there are certain dangers while serving in the military that women must diligently remain aware of for the protection and safety of their mind, body, soul and spirit. It allows you to explore this Ready- Preparedness mindset that a woman must possess; persistence to preserve self, foremostly, while serving in any branch of the military. This will allow others to enter into the demanding new military life, with power of knowledge and the understanding that it is ok to be alarmed of these dangers because I've learned that knowledge is power against these dangers. As a US Army Signal Soldier, (72ECO) Teletype Communication Ops was my MOS (job). I was stationed at 7th Infantry Division, Ft Ord California. I was able to achieve an honorary letter for serving on the HHQ 7th Infantry Division's Public Address Team. I'm currently working on my first book of accountings of my marriage that will be published in January 2023.

I am always advocating for military conduct protocol reform.

For further resource, guided website information please visit my web page:

https://www.voicesofwomenveterans.com

18

BREAKING FREE

Inez Moutarde

U.S. Army Veteran

Just after turning 19, I signed up to join the United States Army Reserves. The opportunity to do military on a part-time basis appealed to me. Mixing military and civilian life as a young person was ideal as I navigated adulthood living independently. The military instilled in me discipline, purpose, responsibility and other than my husband and kids, it is my greatest source of pride.

I joined the military to become a Civil Affairs Specialist. Being in Civil Affairs gave me the opportunities to go on a peacekeeping mission in Bosnia, operational exercise in Egypt, multiple trainings stateside which allowed me to visit places like California, Louisiana, and the Mid-West. I even got to attend Airborne school – Airborne! The military taught me how to have relationships with people, how to overcome challenges, and to work together with people from different backgrounds and cultures.

After September 11th as a Reservist, I knew it was only a matter of time before we'd be activated. I did get that call it was November 28, 2002 - Thanksgiving Day. The alert had been sent and orders were issued not long afterward. Before I knew it, we were at Ft. Bragg getting prepared to head overseas for Operation Iraqi Freedom. This is why I joined the military. I wanted to serve my country and now I had my chance.

Nerves were high amongst everyone, but I started to notice that I was very nonchalant about all of it. I shrugged it off. I couldn't spend too much energy worrying about it as there was too much to do as a Team Sergeant. We arrived in Kuwait in early January 2003. We waited in Kuwait until heading into Iraq in March. It was a very long, tiring tour. We never knew when we were going to go home. Our home dates kept shifting until it was an official 365 days of boots on the ground. Even after that came out, we knew not to get too excited until we were actually home.

In those last few months in Iraq, I realized I felt nothing. Perhaps it was from fatigue but if something horrible happened such as an attack on a vehicle, mortar attack on camp, or even someone dying, I was apathetic. It would be a tragic event, but it didn't tug at my heart.

Detached.

I don't remember.

I closed most of it out.

Then I felt like a jerk for not feeling anything but just keeping it all within.

God forbid we talk about it in any sort of meaningful way.

Suck it up and drive on, right?

Resilience is definitely something you leave the military with.

Being deployed, I earned a Bronze Star for my efforts. Fragmented memories, like a faded dream. I remember parts of being under mortar attack, or nearly getting run over by a tank, hot long days conducting female body searches during chaotic propane tank distributions to locals, handing out eggs to villagers in an effort to win hearts and minds, witnessing riots over electric cuts- all in a day's work. I still haven't shaken the demoralizing feeling of crapping in a field with only a poncho for a shield or having to urinate in a bottle in a moving vehicle in front of my male team members because it was not safe to pull over. Even to this day when I arrive somewhere new, I look for where the toilet is.

My tour ended finally in January 2004, and I was stateside again. My time as a Civil Affairs Specialist in the United States Army Reserves was up. Despite initially wanting to put in a full 20 years to the military, I did not re-enlist. Ten years was enough. I was not the same person. I decided to pack up and move abroad. This Staff Sergeant done with the military for good!

After Iraq there were a lot of people I knew that struggled with PTSD. I didn't. There was suicide, alcoholism, drug abuse, divorces amongst people I knew. These were tragic stories to me, but I didn't feel anything. When the topic of PTSD with old Army friends came up, I didn't get it. In Iraq I had my friends, my team, interesting projects to work on and people with the same sense of humor to keep us going through it all. Why were people I know suffering from PTSD, but I wasn't? I would joke that my childhood was so bad – that there was no room for PTSD from Iraq.

Years later I would come to learn that it there was so much truth in that statement. I had learned long before joining the military how to bury any true feelings.

Flatline Inez – that is what my husband jokingly called me because I didn't ever get too excited about things. It was true. I didn't get too sad, and I never got too excited for anything. It became a running joke whether I loved something or if I hated it - I acted exactly the same which was no emotion. FLATLINE. At least we could laugh about it. But it would take some convincing that if I said I liked something that I truly did, and I wasn't just being sarcastic.

Little did we know it was a coping and defense mechanism I developed from childhood. You see, the military gives me a reference because I remembered what I said. I joked that my childhood was worse than any PTSD from the military.

Just to give a glimpse, I grew up in a very strict household where yelling and shouting were the norm. That is just how we talked to each other. I was raised by a young, single mother and I was the oldest of three. She divorced my father when I was a baby, so I never really got a chance to know him. My mother lived in stress mode, as one would expect a single mother of three to be. Her short temper always kept me on edge. I grew up walking on eggshells as not to set her off – doing my best to make her happy. This created a people pleaser out of me.

I saw her as a lost soul herself, carrying her own childhood trauma into our lives. I witnessed her go through evangelical religious periods which lasted years and made life so restrictive for us as children;

intermittent periods of alcoholism, followed by periods of sobriety. Through it all the physical and emotional abuse was consistent. These cycles remained the same throughout my childhood. I never knew what would piss my mom off, but I worked hard so that it wouldn't happen.

She wasn't always angry or stressed. If you caught my mom on a good day, it was magical. She would be the nicest person and you could have a good laugh, but all it took was one little thing and poof entire mood is shifted.

Despite the rough upbringing, I still sought acknowledgement from her that I was doing good. This continued into adulthood until I became a mother myself. The result of my childhood created a strong desire to create a different life for myself. But the emotional damage left me a person who struggled with confidence, had trust issues, who on occasion drank way too much, was a super people pleaser and knew how to shut down feelings never letting anyone know the REAL me.

As someone who experienced childhood trauma, the military was a good place for me. There is an order to things. You are told what to do, what to wear, and there are very clear guidelines to follow. It becomes a safe place – even if you are in the midst of war. In the journey to unbreaking the chains around myself I can see this clearly.

Despite aiming to make a life different from my childhood, I realized that I was reliving generational trauma. Years later, in spite of having a supportive husband and three amazing children I would find myself dealing with depression hard. I was a ball of negativity which played out in how I acted towards my family, and how I felt emotionally and physically. I felt sick, sad, and numb. Sometimes angry, most times resentful. I was surviving day by day. I hated me. I was failing as a mother, and I hated my life. I hated that I could not shift out of the negative. Even on a good day, it wouldn't take much to set me off into a negative spiral. Whilst I was aiming to be positive, I saw negativity in everything.

I got to a point where I decided enough was enough. I went to see a doctor. He did blood work and made some recommendations but in the end, I chose to deal with this holistically. It was time to make some big changes in my life. What had initially started as a search for inner happiness led me on a deep journey of discovery, healing, and recovery.

I was undoing the chain around my heart and my soul. Little by little discovering more about myself. Then I uncovered something big. I was reliving the same experience of motherhood that my mother had despite us being in two completely different circumstances. She was a young single mother of 3 who was always tired, stressed, angry, lonely, resentful. I don't think she enjoyed motherhood and saw **everything** as a burden. I was married, in my 40's, didn't have the same financial strains, yet here I was repeating the same cycle. I was angry, resentful, stressed - all the same things. I definitely wasn't enjoying motherhood. How horrible is that? I had these three beautiful children that were a handful but, all I could do was be negative most of the time, always quick to anger and in a bit of a victim mode – you know because I HAD to do EVERYTHING for everyone. That is not how I wanted to experience motherhood. This was learned behavior from nearly 30 years beforehand deep inside my system. It was time to break that chain.

I worked with coaches. I delved deep into books from Dr. Joe Dispenza, Dr. Michael Bernard Beckwith, Br. Bruce Lipton, Lisa Nichols, Mel Robbins, Gabby Bernstein – anything that had to do with personal development, I was into it. I focused hard on changing my thought patterns, monitoring what I was thinking all day long, changing up the "I am not enough" story I had been telling myself for years.

One thing I learned from Dr. Joe Dispenza which was pivotal: you must change up your thought process for different results. When you have the same thoughts, this leads to the same choices which lead to the same actions and behaviors leading to the same feeling which leads to the same experience. Everything stays the same. We operate 95% from an automatic behavior. This behavior is learned from those who raised us. Making a conscious choice to change my thinking slowly let to different choices, different actions and behaviors, different feelings. My experience of life was changing. I was breaking that chain.

This was period of my life that was messy, emotional, exhausting. There was so much growing happening during this time. Some days when I felt on top of the world and days when I just reverted to the old ways. So many times, I had to reset, refocus and restart. I was learning to love myself through the process choosing progress over perfection. This work takes consistent daily commitment to experience change.

In summer of 2020 I found Quantum Flow. Quantum Flow is a modality that rewires our entire nervous system. It is a way to break from limiting beliefs that have been holding us back because of the traumas stuck in our body. It works on a physical, energetic, mental, and emotional level. The physical practice includes movements, sounds, breath flow, spirals, posture alignment through which the body is a vehicle of transformation and manifestation. I had made so much progress with the mindset work, but this Quantum Flow practice was a game changer for me. It helped me let go of so much anger and resentment. It brought back strong feeling and emotion into my system.

I am no longer Flatline Inez. My heart is open, I am soul led and inspired. I feel big emotions now. I'm still learning to love myself more, but I have experienced that when you start to love yourself, magic starts happening. You open yourself up to all possibilities which lead to divine synchronicities that become part of the life that you create.

Life still hands me challenges but what is different is how I react to those challenges. Healing is part of the journey. I release anything negative that comes up. I am able to show up for myself and my family in a way that is full of love. The things that used to trigger me no longer do. The way I used to behave seems so foreign to me. I can hold clear boundaries around my space which is something I was never able to do.

Now, only now do I feel the emotion that was missing from Iraq. All the people we lost. All the families effected on all sides. The struggles, the broken families, suicides, all these tragedies that veterans deal with returning home. My own family did not escape this as my Uncle Joe died in Iraq on December 4, 2004.

There is no one and done solution when it comes to healing. You can do all the affirmations, do all the journaling, do all the things but you need to face what is triggering you, go through it, acknowledge it and release. *You've got to feel to heal.* You are here to heal you. It's part of your journey. It's why you are here. Don't let the chains of your past, your trauma hold you back any more. You are here to break free. Say YES to that!

My Chain Breaking Words for You:

There is a life-force within your soul, seek that life. There is a gem in the mountain of your body, seek that mine. O traveler, if you are in search of that, don't look outside, look inside yourself and seek that.

~ Rumi ~

About Inez Moutarde

Margarita Inez Moutarde served in the United States Army Reserves from 1994 until 2004 as a Civil Affair Specialist. When she left the military, she spent nearly two decades living abroad. She lived in the United Kingdom, United Arab Emirates and Switzerland. She currently resides in upstate New York with her husband and 3 children.

She is always spending time with her family but when she does get a moment to herself, she loves running, writing, hiking and cooking.

Her background is in Health and Wellness. She is a Certified Health Coach, Life Coach and a Quantum Flow Practitioner. Quantum Flow is what she is most passionate about. It is an embodiment method that works on every layer of your being, resetting the entire nervous system. She is committed to empowering people through wellness. Guiding people with Quantum Flow to push past limiting beliefs holding them back and to know, feel and experience that the healing power is in them.

19

BREAKING THE CIRCLE OF SILENCE

Gina Baker Alderman

U.S. Navy Veteran

The Phone rings.

"Hello?"

"Gina, this is the XO."

"Hello, Sir. Is everything okay?"

"Gina, we found the CO. He killed himself last night."

Immediately, I begin to cry. I can't believe our Commanding Officer committed suicide. Oh my god. He has a wife and two children. "Sir, what are we going to tell his wife?"

That day has haunted me for 28 years. It made me feel helpless. It made me feel vulnerable. It made me feel weak. I thought if an educated senior military leader could take his own life, what hope did the rest of us have to face life when things got really, really hard? He was our leader, our protector, our pseudo-father. HOW would we survive without him?

The next two weeks after that tragic day were some of the worst stresses I had ever experienced in my entire life. I had to identify the CO's body at the morgue. I had to be present at the funeral home where I saw him laying out dead and naked. I had to help dress him in his military dress blues. I had to drive his car back to the base. I had to face my Sailors and Marines and motivate them to continue doing their jobs. I had to work closely with the CO's wife while planning the funeral for her husband. Worst of all I had to meet with the Naval Criminal Investigative Services who were digging into the CO's personal life and picking it apart piece by piece.

What stress did that man face that would lead him to take his life? The truth is that he was scheduled to meet with the Commanding General the next day and was going to be relieved of Command. The only suitable answer I could conceive for the reason our CO killed himself was that he felt so heartbroken over the thought of being relieved of command that he could not go on living with that grief.

How does a person become so broken that they will take their own life instead of facing the consequences of living? The only thing I could think was the deep and profound suffering a person must experience such as the feelings of agony, misery, desolation, heartbrokenness, and wretchedness. Sitting and thinking how each of those words made me feel allowed me to have a very small glimpse into what my CO might have felt on that tragic day.

The "circle of silence" within our Battalion was deafening. The unsaid words screamed to be released. The grief was all encompassing as each day passed. There was no joy going in to work, only drudgery. It was forbidden to speak about the events that led up to and immediately after the CO's suicide except to officials. We each stuffed our feelings back into our subconscious, learning how to compartmentalize them from the mission we had to achieve. The enlisted personnel did not trust the officers. They voiced that we had betrayed them and our CO. The officers felt betrayed by the superiors in our chain of command. We were not allowed to explain to our troops there had been an investigation and the Commanding General was planning to relieve the CO of Command. The sense of mistrust was strong. Every person in that Battalion was traumatized and silently living in their own personal torment.

How did this affect me personally? My story of trauma is tied directly to my Commanding Officer's suicide. You see, I let that one horrible event in my life haunt me. It haunted me day and night. That horrible event along with childhood trauma haunted me so profoundly over the next 10 years until I was eventually diagnosed with Complex-Post Traumatic Stress Disorder (C-PTSD).

What is C-PTSD? Typically, Post Traumatic Stress Disorder (PTSD) is a reaction to one traumatic incident as the person experiences flashbacks, nightmares, severe anxiety, hypervigilance, and the general inability to regulate emotions and to have healthy relationships. Unlike PTSD, C-PTSD generally begins in childhood and can create a feeling of lack of safety throughout life. A person with C-PTSD has all the symptoms of PTSD, but they can also experience feelings of anger, negative self-image, and disconnection from others. A child who is betrayed by their primary caregiver, another significant family member, or who experienced sexual trauma can bring feelings of mistrust and lack of safety into adulthood. Along with the general population, Active Duty and Military Veterans can experience Complex-Post Traumatic Stress Disorder (C-PTSD). The feelings associated with C-PTSD can often lead to substance abuse, addiction, domestic violence, self-harm, depression, anxiety, attachment disorders and other severe life-altering conditions.

How has C-PTSD impacted my life? C-PTSD has caused me neurological mind-body problems, repeated chest pain, high anxiety, depression, anger issues, lack of trust with romantic partners, difficulty maintaining personal friendships, workaholism, and a video-gaming-addiction. As a result, I have experienced divorce, been admitted to the hospital for medical workups numerous times, lost personal friendships, and experienced financial risk. I developed low self-esteem and a general feeling of low well-being. I had little to no life goals and a general lack of joy. But I found hope!

How did I overcome C-PTSD? There are no quick-fix, overnight cure or one-size fits all method. It is simply constant, relentless work to stay in a positive headspace and to keep myself fully fit emotionally and physically. Fortunately, for the past 15 years I have had a supportive and loving husband who has helped me learn to trust him, to recognize my propensity toward workaholism, and to seek help for my video-gaming-addiction. I also have had supportive counselors who have used tools like hypnosis, cognitive therapy and talk therapy to help ease my suffering. I currently have a wonderful Play Life Coach Brandi Miles and a precious Literary Agent, Publisher and Mentor Sheila Farr who are helping me live my dreams of creating a Veteran Nonprofit and becoming a published author. I am actively working on creating and maintaining solid relationships by setting and reinforcing healthy boundaries. I have also learned how to avoid toxic relationships and to eliminate unhealthy people from my life. To overcome C-PTSD I found I must work every day of my life toward maintaining a health mind, body and spirit.

What else have I done to overcome my C-PTSD? This last 14 months I have made a significant effort to seek a closer relationship with God and His Son, Jesus Christ. Becoming a Christian at the age of 12 provided a spiritual foundation throughout my life that allowed me to have hope, peace, and joy. When I was at my lowest points in life and thinking about suicide I reached out to God, and He sent His Holy Spirit to love me and comfort me. Often when I felt completely broken and cried out to God and asking Him to take my burden, He immediately answered my prayers. The greatest gift of my life has been having God and His Holy Bible actively in my life. There is no doubt in my mind that without God I would not be alive today.

Did my suffering end? No, it did not end, but I gained a whole new perspective over how I looked at suffering. Over the twenty-eight years since my CO killed himself, God has helped me realize suffering is a natural part of life. As life unfolds people get disease, experience divorces, lose jobs, family members die along with so many other tragic events. For me, the answer about suffering is how we choose to live with it, and embrace it, so that it does not interfere with living a healthy and happy life.

How can YOU overcome suffering? The Women Veteran Authors in this book understand that trauma and suffering can make you feel alone, isolated, desolated, broken, hopeless, helpless and much more....but, we want you to know YOU ARE NOT ALONE! Every woman in this book has felt the deepest depths of despair and each one of us found hope. You can find hope too!

What can you do to feel better? First, when you are feeling down and having bad thoughts try to interrupt your thoughts.

Think of a STOP sign. S = Stop. T = Thoughts. O = On. and P = Purpose.

Say the word STOP inside your mind or out loud.

Next, replace that thought with an activity and a pleasant thought. An activity could include taking a bath or shower, or you could walk inside or outside of your house. Get up from where you are sitting and act. While you are moving change your thoughts of despair into thoughts of the power you hold within yourself. You are good enough! You are loved! You have greatness inside of yourself! You have the power inside yourself to connect with others! You can connect to God by a simple prayer of "help." You can connect to another human being by making one phone call and simply asking for "help." All you have to do is to reach out. Do not sit in your misery. Right now, reach out and say these words, "Lord, I need help. I need help right now." Or make that phone call and tell them, "I need help. I need help right now."

Your first instinct might be to run away. You may have heard of the self-preservation "fight or flight" instinct when a person is faced with difficulty. Our instinct in our mind tells us to either stand our ground and fight, or to flee the situation. Running away into suicide is not the answer, although you may want to run away with every fiber of your being. Ending your life is in essence a form of running away from life. STOP those thoughts right now.

The National Suicide Prevention Lifeline is available 24 hours at 1-800-273-8255. This is a free and confidential support center for people in distress. The phones are manned by trained crisis workers. They will listen to you, understand how your problem is affecting you, provide you support, and get you the help you need. The Veteran's crisis line is the same number, and you access it by pressing "one."

You can break free of the chain of suffering and trauma. You can end the "circle of silence" in your life! I believe in you! Our Women in this book believe in you! God believes in you!

My Chain Breaking Words for You:

You are not alone! In your deepest darkest hours of despair God is there. God has a plan for You! In the holy anointed Bible John 3:16 tells us, "God loves us so much that He gave us His one and only son, Jesus Christ, and whoever believes in Him will have ever lasting eternal life." Jesus Christ tells us in John 10:10, "I came that they may have life and have it abundantly." Each of us are sinners and we have been separated from God through the fall of man and our failure to obey Him and living sinful lives. The Bible tells us in Romans 3:23, "All have sinned and fall short of the glory of God." Romans 6:23 tells us that the result of sin is death and results in spiritual separation from God. God gave us hope for a future and Romans 5:8 tells us, "God demonstrates His own love toward us, in that while we were yet sinners, Christ died for us." The "good news" is that Jesus "Christ died for our sins. ... He was buried. ... He was raised on the third day, according to the Scriptures" (1 Corinthians 15:3-4). Jesus said in John 14:6, "I am the way, and the truth, and the life; no one comes to the Father, but through me."

What do you need to do to have God actively in your life? Believe you are loved and accepted by God; pray to God, acknowledging your sins and ask forgiveness for those sins, and turn from your sins. Here is a prayer you can pray to accept Jesus Christ as your Savior: "Dear God, I know I am a sinner, and I ask for your forgiveness. I believe Jesus Christ is Your Son. I believe that He died for my sin and that you raised Him to life. I want to trust Him as my Savior and follow Him as Lord, from this day forward. Guide my life and help me to do your will. I pray this in the name of Jesus. Amen."

To learn more about God and Jesus Christ I recommend the following website from Billy Graham Evangelistic Association: www.PeaceWithGod.net and www.PeaceWithGod.net/mobile/

About Gina Baker Alderman

Gina Baker Alderman is a life-long military Veteran advocate. As CEO and founder of Rugged Warrior Healing Coalition, Gina is passionate about easing Veteran suffering.

As visionary author and leader of the Veterans Unchained book series, Gina provides a healing outlet and hope for those impacted by trauma.

Gina served active duty and retired from the US Navy after 28 years' service as a Hospital Administrator with a wartime specialty of Medical Plans and Operations.

When she's not volunteering or working on Veteran causes, you can find Gina at home in Tampa, Florida with her husband and two French Bulldogs, or off riding her Harley Davidson Triglide Ultra Trike.

You can connect with Gina through FaceBook or Linkedin.

Facebook: https://www.facebook.com/Rugged-Warrior-Healing-Coalition-111745114754044/

Linkedin: https://www.linkedin.com/in/gina-alderman-4a5b619b

RESOURCES

Department of Defense Safe Helpline

Safe Helpline is the DOD's sole hotline for members of the DOD community affected by sexual assault. Completely anonymous, confidential, 24/7, specialized service – providing help and information anytime, anywhere. A Safe Helpline user can access one-on-one support, peer-to-peer support, information, resources, and selfcare exercises to aid in their recovery.

https://www.hotline.safehelpline.org

Call: 877-995-5247

Text: 55247

Mission 22

Mission 22 supports active-duty military, Veterans, and their families nation-wide. They have three areas of focus. One arm of support includes Post-Traumatic Stress, Traumatic Brain Injury, and suicide risk. Resources are provided to monitor and evaluate stress, sleep, and activity levels; includes meditation and coaching; integrates exercise and wellness programs; and provides education resources. A second area of support includes connecting the civilian and military communities to raise awareness of issues unique to military members and their families. A third area of focus is Mission 22's memorial support. Through this support service members and Veterans are remembered and honored through large scale installations and digital initiatives. Through Mission 22's Ambassador program a network of more than 3,500 Veterans and civilians in all 50 states and around the world work to advance understanding of unique issues and challenges faced by active service members, Veterans, and their families.

https://www.mission22.com

Call: 503-908-8505

National Domestic Violence Hotline

24/7 access to resources and support specifically aimed at teen and adult relationships. This hotline can help you create an interactive safety plan and to build a future without fear. Your safety plan is designed as a personalized, practical plan to improve your safety while experiencing abuse, preparing to leave an abusive situation, or after you leave. Contact this resource to have a highly trained advocate help you prepare your personalized safety plan.

https://www.thehotline.org

Call: 800-799-7233

Text: START to 88788

National Suicide Prevention Lifeline

Veteran's Crisis Line -- same number and to access it press "one" on your phone.

The Lifeline provides 24/7, free and confidential support for people in distress, prevention and crisis resources for you or your loved ones, and best practices for professionals in the United States.

https://suicidepreventionlifeline.org

Call: 800-273-8255

Made in the USA
Columbia, SC
29 October 2023

25165497R00095